The Poems
of Alice Meynell

The Poems
of Alice Meynell

1847—1923

CENTENARY EDITION

London
Hollis and Carter
1947

PRINTED IN GREAT BRITAIN
AT THE CHISWICK PRESS
NEW SOUTHGATE
LONDON, N.11

EDITOR'S NOTE

ALICE MEYNELL esteemed the poetry of her middle and later years beyond that of her girlhood; a judgement with which the present editor concurs out of more than filial piety. Therefore he places first in the book, according to her known wish, the poems of her maturity and age. These are followed by her early poems, here arranged in three divisions: those which she herself wished, or was persuaded, to reprint in her first Collected Edition (1913); those which, though printed in *Preludes* (1875) or in periodicals, she later rejected from "collected" editions; and those which she herself refrained from publishing, but which were retrieved from an early MS for the Oxford edition of 1940. To these very early pieces I think her readers have a right which the order of this book reconciles with my mother's right to the clear labelling of them as self-rejected. In some instances they will add to her stature as a poet, in most as a critic.

There are two poems which defy these categories. *Renouncement* was written before 1875, but not printed till 1882 nor collected till 1893; *Singers to Come* was printed in a magazine in 1877 but not collected till 1893. I place them where Alice Meynell chose to place them, out of their time.

FRANCIS MEYNELL

CONTENTS

first printed in *Preludes*, 1875, and
chosen by the author for reprinting in *Collected Poems*, 1913.

POEMS 1893-1923

Renouncement

I MUST not think of thee; and, tired yet strong,
   I shun the thought that lurks in all delight—
   The thought of thee—and in the blue Heaven's height,
And in the sweetest passage of a song.
Oh, just beyond the fairest thoughts that throng
   This breast, the thought of thee waits hidden yet bright;
   But it must never, never come in sight;
I must stop short of thee the whole day long.

But when sleep comes to close each difficult day,
   When night gives pause to the long watch I keep,
      And all my bonds I needs must loose apart,
Must doff my will as raiment laid away—
   With the first dream that comes with the first sleep
      I run, I run, I am gathered to thy heart.

No new delights to our desire
   The singers of the past can yield.
   I lift mine eyes to hill and field,
And see in them your yet dumb lyre,
   Poets unborn and unrevealed.

Singers to come, what thoughts will start
   To song? What words of yours be sent
   Through man's soul, and with earth be blent?
These worlds of nature and the heart
   Await you like an instrument.

Who knows what musical flocks of words
   Upon these pine-tree tops will light,
   And crown these towers in circling flight,
And cross these seas like summer birds,
   And give a voice to the day and night?

Something of you already is ours;
   Some mystic part of you belongs
To us whose dreams your future throngs,
Who look on hills, and trees, and flowers,
   Which will mean so much in your songs.

I wonder, like the maid who found,
   And knelt to lift, the lyre supreme
   Of Orpheus from the Thracian stream.
She dreams on its sealed past profound;
   On a deep future sealed I dream.

14

She bears it in her wanderings
   Within her arms, and has not pressed
   Her unskilled fingers but her breast
Upon those silent sacred strings;
   I, too, clasp mystic strings at rest.

For I, in the world of lands and seas,
   The sky of wind and rain and fire,
   And in man's world of long desire—
In all that is yet dumb in these—
   Have found a more mysterious lyre.

The Moon to the Sun

The Poet sings to her Poet

As the full moon shining there
To the sun that lighteth her
Am I unto thee for ever,
O my secret glory-giver!
O my light, I am dark but fair,
　　Black but fair.

Shine, Earth loves thee! And then shine
And be loved through thoughts of mine
All thy secrets that I treasure
I translate them at my pleasure.
I am crowned with glory of thine:
　　Thine, not thine.

I make pensive thy delight,
And thy strong gold silver-white.
Though all beauty of mine thou makest,
Yet to earth which thou forsakest
I have made thee fair all night,
　　Day all night.

16

Unlinked

IF I should quit thee, sacrifice, forswear,
    To what, my art, shall I give thee in keeping?
    To the long winds of heaven? Shall these come sweeping
My songs forgone against my face and hair?
Or shall the mountain streams my lost joys bear,
    My past poetic pain in rain be weeping?
    No, I shall live a poet waking, sleeping,
And I shall die a poet unaware.

From me, my art, thou canst not pass away;
    And I, a singer though I cease to sing,
        Shall own thee without joy in thee or woe.
Through my indifferent words of every day,
    Scattered and all unlinked the rhymes shall ring,
        And make my poem; and I shall not know.

A Song of Derivations

I COME from nothing; but from where
Come the undying thoughts I bear?
  Down, through long links of death and birth,
  From the past poets of the earth,
My immortality is there.

I am like the blossom of an hour.
But long, long vanished sun and shower
  Awoke my breath in the young world's air;
  I track the past back everywhere
Through seed and flower and seed and flower.

Or I am like a stream that flows
Full of the cold springs that arose
  In morning lands, in distant hills;
  And down the plain my channel fills
With melting of forgotten snows.

Voices I have not heard, possessed
My own fresh songs; my thoughts are blessed
  With relics of the far unknown.
  And mixed with memories not my own
The sweet streams throng into my breast.

Before this life began to be,
The happy songs that wake in me
  Woke long ago and far apart.
  Heavily on this little heart
Presses their immortality.

After a Parting

Farewell has long been said; I have forgone thee;
  I never name thee even.
But how shall I learn virtues and yet shun thee?
  For thou art so near Heaven
That Heavenward meditations pause upon thee.

Thou dost beset the path to every shrine;
  My trembling thoughts discern
Thy goodness in the good for which I pine;
  And, if I turn from but one sin, I turn
Unto a smile of thine.

How shall I thrust thee apart
  Since all my growth tends to thee night and day—
To thee faith, hope, and art?
  Swift are the currents setting all one way;
They draw my life, my life, out of my heart.

Veni Creator

So humble things Thou hast borne for us, O God,
Left'st Thou a path of lowliness untrod?
Yes, one, till now, another Olive-Garden.
For we endure the tender pain of pardon:
One with another we forbear. Give heed,
Look at the mournful world Thou hast decreed.
The time has come. At last we hapless men
Know all our haplessness all through. Come, then,
Endure undreamed humility: Lord of Heaven,
Come to our ignorant hearts and be forgiven.

The Shepherdess

SHE walks—the lady of my delight—
    A shepherdess of sheep.
Her flocks are thoughts. She keeps them white;
    She guards them from the steep;
She feeds them on the fragrant height,
    And folds them in for sleep.

She roams maternal hills and bright,
    Dark valleys safe and deep.
Into that tender breast at night
    The chastest stars may peep.
She walks—the lady of my delight—
    A shepherdess of sheep.

She holds her little thoughts in sight,
    Though gay they run and leap.
She is so circumspect and right;
    She has her soul to keep.
She walks—the lady of my delight—
    A shepherdess of sheep.

'I am the Way'

THOU art the Way.
  Hadst Thou been nothing but the goal,
I cannot say
If Thou hadst ever met my soul.

I cannot see—
I, child of process—if there lies
  An end for me,
Full of repose, full of replies.

I'll not reproach
The road that winds, my feet that err.
  Access, Approach
Art Thou, Time, Way, and Wayfarer.

Via, et Veritas, et Vita

'Y ou never attained to Him?' 'If to attain
        Be to abide, then that may be.'
'Endless the way, followed with how much pain!'
            'The way was He.'

'Why wilt thou Chide?'

WHY wilt thou chide,
   Who hast attained to be denied?
    O learn, above
All price is my refusal, Love.
    My sacred Nay
Was never cheapened by the way.
Thy single sorrow crowns thee lord
Of an unpurchasable word.

    O strong, O pure!
As Yea makes happier loves secure,
    I vow thee this
Unique rejection of a kiss.
    I guard for thee
This jealous sad monopoly.
I seal this honour thine; none dare
Hope for a part in thy despair.

The Lady Poverty

THE Lady Poverty was fair:
  But she has lost her looks of late,
With change of times and change of air.
Ah slattern! she neglects her hair,
Her gown, her shoes; she keeps no state
As once when her pure feet were bare.

Or—almost worse, if worse can be—
She scolds in parlours, dusts and trims,
Watches and counts. Oh, is this she
Whom Francis met, whose step was free,
Who with Obedience carolled hymns,
In Umbria walked with Chastity?

Where is her ladyhood? Not here,
Not among modern kinds of men;
But in the stony fields, where clear
Through the thin trees the skies appear,
In delicate spare soil and fen,
And slender landscape and austere.

Parentage

> 'When Augustus Cæsar legislated against the
> unmarried citizens of Rome, he declared them
> to be, in some sort, slayers of the people.'

Ah no! not these!
These, who were childless, are not they who
  gave
So many dead unto the journeying wave,
The helpless nurslings of the cradling seas;
Not they who doomed by infallible decrees
Unnumbered man to the innumerable grave.

But those who slay
Are fathers. Theirs are armies. Death is theirs—
The death of innocences and despairs;
The dying of the golden and the grey.
The sentence, when these speak it, has no Nay.
And she who slays is she who bears, who bears.

The Fold

BEHOLD,
  The time is now! Bring back, bring back
Thy flocks of fancies, wild of whim.
Oh, lead them from the mountain-track,
    Thy frolic thoughts untold.
Oh, bring them in—the fields grow dim—
    And let me be the fold!

Behold,
The time is now! Call in, oh, call
Thy pasturing kisses gone astray
For scattered sweets; gather them all
    To shelter from the cold.
Throng them together, close and gay,
    And let me be the fold!

Cradle-Song at Twilight

THE child not yet is lulled to rest.
 Too young a nurse, the slender Night
So laxly holds him to her breast
 That throbs with flight.

He plays with her, and will not sleep.
 For other playfellows she sighs;
An unmaternal fondness keep
 Her alien eyes.

The Roaring Frost

A FLOCK of winds came winging from the North,
Strong birds with fighting pinions driving forth
    With a resounding call:—

Where will they close their wings and cease their cries—
Between what warming seas and conquering skies—
    And fold, and fall?

To W. M.

HOME, home from the horizon far and clear,
        Hither the soft wings sweep;
Flocks of the memories of the day draw near
        The dovecote doors of sleep.

Oh, which are they that come through sweetest light
        Of all these homing birds?
Which with the straightest and the swiftest flight?
        Your words to me, your words!

Oh, what a kiss
     With filial passion overcharged is this!
          To this misgiving breast
This child runs, as a child ne'er ran to rest
Upon the light heart and the unoppressed.

          Unhoped, unsought!
A little tenderness, this mother thought
          The utmost of her meed.
She looked for gratitude; content indeed
With thus much that her nine years' love had bought.

          Nay, even with less.
This mother, giver of life, death, peace, distress,
          Desired ah! not so much
Thanks as forgiveness; and the passing touch
Expected, and the slight, the brief caress.

          O filial light
Strong in these childish eyes, these new, these bright
          Intelligible stars! Their rays
Are near the constant earth, guides in the maze,
Natural, true, keen in this dusk of days.

ANOTHER day awakes. And who—
Changing the world—is this?
He comes at whiles, the winter through,
    West Wind! I would not miss
His sudden tryst: the long, the new
    Surprises of his kiss.

Vigilant, I make haste to close
    With him who comes my way.
I go to meet him as he goes;
    I know his note, his lay,
His colour and his morning-rose,
    And I confess his day.

My window waits; at dawn I hark
    His call; at morn I meet
His haste around the tossing park
    And down the softened street;
The gentler light is his: the dark,
    The grey—he turns it sweet.

So too, so too do I confess
    My poet when he sings.
He rushes on my mortal guess
    With his immortal things.
I feel, I know, him. On I press—
    He finds me 'twixt his wings.

November Blue

*The golden tint of the electric lights seems
to give a complementary colour to the air
in the early evening:—ESSAY ON LONDON*

O HEAVENLY colour, London town
 Has blurred it from her skies;
And, hooded in an earthly brown,
 Unheaven'd the city lies.
No longer, standard-like, this hue
 Above the broad road flies;
Nor does the narrow street the blue
 Wear, slender pennon-wise.

But when the gold and silver lamps
 Colour the London dew,
And, misted by the winter damps,
 The shops shine bright anew—
Blue comes to earth, it walks the street,
 It dyes the wide air through;
A mimic sky about their feet,
 The throng go crowned with blue.

c

Chimes

BRIEF, on a flying night,
From the shaken tower
A flock of bells take flight,
   And go with the hour.

Like birds from the cote to the gales,
   Abrupt—oh, hark!
A fleet of bells set sails,
   And go to the dark.

Sudden the cold airs swing.
   Alone, aloud,
A verse of bells takes wing
   And flies with the cloud.

Unto us a Son is given

GIVEN, not lent,
And not withdrawn—once sent,
This Infant of mankind, this One,
Is still the little welcome Son.

New every year,
New born and newly dear,
He comes with tidings and a song,
The ages long, the ages long;

Even as the cold
Keen winter grows not old,
As childhood is so fresh, foreseen,
And spring in the familiar green—

Sudden as sweet
Come the expected feet.
All joy is young, and new all art,
And He, too, Whom we have by heart.

A Dead Harvest

In Kensington Gardens

ALONG the graceless grass of town
  They rake the rows of red and brown—
Dead leaves, unlike the rows of hay
Delicate, touched with gold and grey,
Raked long ago and far away.

A narrow silence in the park,
Between the lights a narrow dark.
One street rolls on the north; and one,
Muffled, upon the south doth run;
Amid the mist the work is done.

A futile crop!—for it the fire
Smoulders, and, for a stack, a pyre.
So go the town's lives on the breeze,
Even as the sheddings of the trees;
Bosom nor barn is filled with these.

The Two Poets

WHOSE is the speech
      That moves the voices of this lonely beech?
Out of the long west did this wild wind come—
O strong and silent! And the tree was dumb,
      Ready and dumb, until
The dumb gale struck it on the darkened hill.

      Two memories,
Two powers, two promises, two silences
Closed in this cry, closed in these thousand leaves
Articulate. This sudden hour retrieves
      The purpose of the past,
Separate, apart—embraced, embraced at last.

      'Whose is the word?
Is it I that spake? Is it thou? Is it I that heard?'
'Thine earth was solitary, yet I found thee!'
'Thy sky was pathless, but I caught, I bound thee,
      Thou visitant divine.'
'O thou my Voice, the word was thine.' 'Was thine.'

Thou man, first-comer, whose wide arms entreat,
   Gather, clasp, welcome, bind,
Lack, or remember; whose warm pulses beat
   With love of thine own kind:—

Unlifted for a blessing on yon sea,
   Unshrined on this highway,
O flesh, O grief, thou too shalt have our knee,
   Thou rood of every day!

Luminous passions reign
   High in the soul of man; and they are twain.
Of these he hath made the poetry of earth—
Hath made his nobler tears, his magic mirth.

   Fair Love is one of these,
The visiting vision of seven centuries;
And one is love of Nature—love to tears—
The modern passion of this hundred years.

   Oh, never to such height,
Oh, never to such spiritual light—
The light of lonely visions, and the gleam
Of secret splendid sombre suns in dream—

   Oh, never to such long
Glory in life, supremacy in song,
Had either of these loves attained in joy,
But for the ministration of a boy.

   Dante was one who bare
Love in his deep heart, apprehended there
When he was yet a child; and from that day
The radiant love has never passed away.

   And one was Wordsworth; he
Conceived the love of Nature childishly
As no adult heart might; old poets sing
That exaltation by remembering.

   For no divine
Intelligence, or art, or fire, or wine,
Is high-delirious as that rising lark—
The child's soul and its daybreak in the dark.

And Letters keep these two
Heavenly treasures safe the ages through,
Safe from ignoble benison or ban—
These two high childhoods in the heart of man.

To Sylvia two years old

LONG life to thee, long virtue, long delight,
  A flowering early and late!
Long beauty, grave to thought and gay to sight,
  A distant date!

Yet, as so many poets love to sing
  (When young the child will die),
'No autumn will destroy this lovely spring,'
  So, Sylvia, I.

I'll write thee dapper verse and touching rhyme;
  'Our eyes shall not behold—'
The commonplace shall serve for thee this time:
  'Never grow old.'

For there's another way to stop thy clock
  Within my cherishing heart,
To carry thee unalterable, and lock
  Thy youth apart:

Thy flower, for me, shall evermore be hid
  In this close bud of thine,
Not, Sylvia, by thy death—O God forbid!
  Merely by mine.

Saint Catherine of Siena

Written for Strephon, who said that a woman must
lean, or she should not have his chivalry

THE light young man who was to die,
    Stopped in his frolic by the State,
Aghast, beheld the world go by;
    But Catherine crossed his dungeon gate.

She found his lyric courage dumb,
    His stripling beauties strewn in wrecks,
His modish bravery overcome;
    Small profit had he of his sex.

On any old wife's level he,
    For once—for all. But he alone—
Man—must not fear the mystery,
    The pang, the passage, the unknown:

Death. He did fear it, in his cell,
    Darkling amid the Tuscan sun;
And, weeping, at her feet he fell,
    The sacred, young, provincial nun.

She prayed, she preached him innocent;
    She gave him to the Sacrificed;
On her courageous breast he leant,
    The breast where beat the heart of Christ.

He left it for the block, with cries
    Of victory on his severed breath.
That crimson head she clasped, her eyes
    Blind with the splendour of his death.

42

And will the man of modern years
  —Stern on the Vote—withhold from thee,
Thou prop, thou cross, erect, in tears,
  Catherine, the service of his knee?

The Watershed

Written between Munich and Verona

BLACK mountains pricked with pointed pine
A melancholy sky.
Out-distanced was the German vine,
The sterile fields lay high.
From swarthy Alps I travelled forth
Aloft; it was the north, the north;
Bound for the Noon was I.

I seemed to breast the streams that day;
I met, opposed, withstood
The northward rivers on their way,
My heart against the flood—
My heart that pressed to rise and reach,
And felt the love of altering speech,
Of frontiers, in its blood.

But oh, the unfolding South! the burst
Of summer! Oh, to see
Of all the southward brooks the first!
The travelling heart went free
With endless streams; that strife was stopped;
And down a thousand vales I dropped,
I flowed to Italy.

The Joyous Wanderer

(after Catulle Mendès)

I GO by road, I go by street—
    Lira, la, la!
O white highways, ye know my feet!
A loaf I carry and, all told,
Three broad bits of lucky gold—
    Lira, la, la!
And oh, within my flowering heart,
(Sing, dear nightingale!) is my Sweet.

A poor man met me and begged for bread—
    Lira, la, la!
'Brother, take all the loaf,' I said,
I shall but go with lighter cheer—
    Lira, la, la!
And oh, within my flowering heart
(Sing, sweet nightingale!) is my Dear.

A thief I met on the lonely way—
    Lira, la, la!
He took my gold; I cried to him, 'Stay!
And take my pocket and make an end.'
    Lira, la, la!
And oh, within my flowering heart
(Sing, soft nightingale!) is my Friend.

Now on the plain I have met with death—
    Lira, la, la!
My bread is gone, my gold, my breath.
But oh, this heart is not afraid—
    Lira, la, la!
For oh, within this lonely heart
(Sing, sad nightingale!) is my Maid.

The Rainy Summer

There's much afoot in heaven and earth this year;
  The winds hunt up the sun, hunt up the moon,
Trouble the dubious dawn, hasten the drear
  Height of a threatening noon.

No breath of boughs, no breath of leaves, of fronds,
  May linger or grow warm; the trees are loud;
The forest, rooted, tosses in her bonds,
  And strains against the cloud.

No scents may pause within the garden-fold;
  The rifled flowers are cold as ocean-shells;
Bees, humming in the storm, carry their cold
  Wild honey to cold cells.

A Poet's Wife

I SAW a tract of ocean locked inland,
  Within a field's embrace—
The very sea! Afar it fled the strand,
  And gave the seasons chase,
And met the night alone, the tempest spanned,
  Saw sunrise face to face.

O Poet, more than ocean, lonelier!
  In inaccessible rest
And storm remote, thou, sea of thoughts, dost stir
  Scattered through east to west,—
Now, while thou closest with the kiss of her
  Who locks thee to her breast.

Messina, 1908

Lord, Thou hast crushed Thy tender ones, o'er-
    thrown
  Thy strong, Thy fair; Thy man thou hast unmanned,
Thy elaborate works unwrought, Thy deeds undone,
  Thy lovely sentient human plan unplanned;
Destroyer, we have cowered beneath Thine own
  Immediate, unintelligible hand.

Lord, Thou hast hastened to retrieve, to heal,
  To feed, to bind, to clothe, to quench the brand,
To prop the ruin, to bless, and to anneal;
  Hast sped Thy ships by sea, Thy trains by land,
Shed pity and tears:—our shattered fingers feel
  Thy mediate and intelligible hand.

ONE of the crowd went up,
And knelt before the Paten and the Cup,
Received the Lord, returned in peace, and prayed
Close to my side. Then in my heart I said:

'O Christ, in this man's life—
This stranger who is Thine—in all his strife,
All his felicity, his good and ill,
In the assaulted stronghold of his will,

'I do confess Thee here,
Alive within this life; I know Thee near
Within this lonely conscience, closed away
Within this brother's solitary day.

'Christ in his unknown heart,
His intellect unknown—this love, this art,
This battle and this peace, this destiny
That I shall never know—look upon me!

'Christ in his numbered breath,
Christ in his beating heart and in his death,
Christ in his mystery! From that secret place
And from that separate dwelling, give me grace!'

A General Communion

I saw the throng, so deeply separate,
  Fed at one only board—
The devout people, moved, intent, elate,
    And the devoted Lord.

O struck apart! not side from human side,
    But soul from human soul,
As each asunder absorbed the multiplied,
    The ever unparted, whole.

I saw this people as a field of flowers,
    Each grown at such a price
The sum of unimaginable powers
    Did no more than suffice.

A thousand single central daisies they,
    A thousand of the one;
For each, the entire monopoly of day;
    For each, the whole of the devoted sun.

The Fugitive

'Nous avons chassé ce Jésus-Christ': FRENCH PUBLICIST

YES, from the ingrate heart, the street
  Of garrulous tongue, the warm retreat
    Within the village and the town;
    Not from the lands where ripen brown
A thousand thousand hills of wheat;

Not from the long Burgundian line,
The Southward, sunward range of vine.
    Hunted, He never will escape
    The flesh, the blood, the sheaf, the grape,
That feed His man—the bread, the wine.

In Portugal, 1912

AND will they cast the altars down,
Scatter the chalice, crush the bread?
In field, in village, and in town
He hides an unregarded head;

Waits in the corn-lands far and near,
Bright in His sun, dark in His frost,
Sweet in the vine, ripe in the ear—
Lonely unconsecrated Host.

In ambush at the merry board
The Victim lurks unsacrificed;
The mill conceals the harvest's Lord,
The wine-press holds the unbidden Christ.

The Crucifixion

OH, man's capacity
        For spiritual sorrow, corporal pain!
Who has explored the deepmost of that sea,
With heavy links of a far-fathoming chain?

        That melancholy lead,
Let down in guilty and in innocent hold,
Yea into childish hands deliverèd,
Leaves the sequestered floor unreached, untold.

        One only has explored
The deepmost; but He did not die of it.
Not yet, not yet He died. Man's human Lord
Touched the extreme; it is not infinite.

        But over the abyss
Of God's capacity for woe He stayed
One hesitating hour; what gulf was this?
Forsaken He went down, and was afraid.

The Newer Vainglory

Two men went up to pray; and one gave thanks,
    Not with himself—aloud,
With proclamation, calling on the ranks
    Of an attentive crowd.

'Thank God, I clap not my own humble breast,
    But other ruffians' backs,
Imputing crime—such is my tolerant haste—
    To any man that lacks.

'For I am tolerant, generous, keep no rules,
    And the age honours me.
Thank God, I am not as these rigid fools,
    Even as this Pharisee.'

In Manchester Square

In Memoriam T. H.

THE paralytic man has dropped in death
    The crossing-sweeper's brush to which he clung,
One-handed, twisted, dwarfed, scanted of breath,
    Although his hair was young.

I saw this year the winter vines of France,
    Dwarfed, twisted goblins in the frosty drouth—
Gnarled, crippled, blackened little stems askance
    On long hills to the South.

Great green and golden hands of leaves ere long
    Shall proffer clusters in that vineyard wide.
And oh, his might, his sweet, his wine, his song,
    His stature, since he died!

Maternity

ONE wept whose only child was dead,
   New-born, ten years ago.
'Weep not; he is in bliss,' they said.
   She answered, 'Even so,

'Ten years ago was born in pain
   A child, not now forlorn.
But oh, ten years ago, in vain,
   A mother, a mother was born.'

The First Snow

NOT yet was winter come to earth's soft floor,
The tideless wave, the warm white road, the shore,
The serried town whose small street tortuously
    Led darkling to the dazzling sea.

Not yet to breathing man, not to his song,
Not to his comforted heart; not to the long
Close-cultivated lands beneath the hill.
    Summer was gently with them still.

But on the Apennine mustered the cloud;
The grappling storm shut down. Aloft, aloud,
Ruled secret tempest one long day and night,
    Until another morning's light.

O tender mountain-tops and delicate,
Where summer-long the westering sunlight sate!
Within that fastness darkened from the sun,
    What solitary things were done?

The clouds let go, they rose, they winged away;
Snow-white the altered mountains faced the day:
As saints who keep their counsel sealed and fast,
    Their anguish over-past.

The Courts

A Figure of the Epiphany

THE poet's imageries are noble ways,
  Approaches to a plot, an open shrine,
Their splendours, colours, avenues, arrays,
    Their courts that run with wine;

Beautiful similes, 'fair and flagrant things,'
Enriched, enamouring,—raptures, metaphors
Enhancing life, are paths for pilgrim kings
    Made free of golden doors.

And yet the open heavenward plot, with dew,
Ultimate poetry, enclosed, enskied,
(Albeit such ceremonies lead thereto)
    Stands on the yonder side.

Plain, behind oracles, it is; and past
All symbols, simple; perfect, heavenly-wild,
The song some loaded poets reach at last—
    The kings that found a Child.

The Launch

FORTH, to the alien gravity,
Forth, to the laws of ocean, we,
　Builders on earth by laws of land,
　Entrust this creature of our hand
Upon the calculated sea.

Fast bound to shore we cling, we creep,
And make our ship ready to leap
　Light to the flood, equipped to ride
　The strange conditions of the tide—
New weight, new force, new world: the Deep.

Ah thus—not thus—the Dying, kissed,
Cherished, exhorted, shriven, dismissed;
　By all the eager means we hold
　We, warm, prepare him for the cold,
To keep the incalculable tryst.

To the Body

THOU inmost, ultimate
　　Council of judgement, palace of decrees,
Where the high senses hold their spiritual state,
　　Sued by earth's embassies,
And sign, approve, accept, conceive, create;

　　Create—thy senses close
With the world's pleas. The random odours reach
Their sweetness in the place of thy repose,
　　Upon thy tongue the peach,
And in thy nostrils breathes the breathing rose.

　　To thee, secluded one,
The dark vibrations of the sightless skies,
The lovely inexplicit colours, run;
　　The light gropes for those eyes.
O thou august! thou dost command the sun.

　　Music, all dumb, hath trod
Into thine ear her one effectual way;
And fire and cold approach to gain thy nod,
　　Where thou call'st up the day,
Where thou awaitest the appeal of God.

The Unexpected Peril

UNLIKE the youth that all men say
    They prize—youth of abounding blood,
In love with the sufficient day,
    And gay in growth, and strong in bud;

Unlike was mine! Then my first slumber
    Nightly rehearsed my last; each breath
Knew itself one of the unknown number.
    But Life was urgent with me as Death.

My shroud was in the flocks; the hill
    Within its quarry locked my stone;
My bier grew in the woods; and still
    Life spurred me where I paused alone.

'Begin!' Life called. Again her shout,
    'Make haste while it is called to-day!'
Her exhortations plucked me out,
    Hunted me, turned me, held me at bay.

But if my youth is thus hard pressed
    (I thought) what of a later year?
If the end so threats this tender breast,
    What of the days when it draws near?

Draws near, and little done? Yet lo,
    Dread has forborne, and haste lies by.
I was beleaguered; now the foe
    Has raised the siege, I know not why.

I see them troop away; I ask
　　Were they in sooth mine enemies—
Terror, the doubt, the lash, the task?
　　What heart has my new housemate, Ease?

How am I left, at last, alive,
　　To make a stranger of a tear?
What did I do one day to drive
　　From me the vigilant angel, Fear?

The diligent angel, Labour? Ay,
　　The inexorable angel, Pain?
Menace me, lest indeed I die,
　　Sloth! Turn; crush, teach me fear again!

Christ in the Universe

WITH this ambiguous earth
His dealings have been told us. These abide:
The signal to a maid, the human birth,
The lesson, and the young Man crucified.

But not a star of all
The innumerable host of stars has heard
How He administered this terrestrial ball.
Our race have kept their Lord's entrusted Word.

Of His earth-visiting feet
None knows the secret, cherished, perilous,
The terrible, shamefast, frightened, whispered, sweet,
Heart-shattering secret of His way with us.

No planet knows that this
Our wayside planet, carrying land and wave,
Love and life multiplied, and pain and bliss,
Bears, as chief treasure, one forsaken grave.

Nor, in our little day,
May His devices with the heavens be guessed,
His pilgrimage to thread the Milky Way,
Or His bestowals there be manifest.

But, in the eternities,
Doubtless we shall compare together, hear
A million alien Gospels, in what guise
He trod the Pleiades, the Lyre, the Bear.

Oh, be prepared, my soul!
To read the inconceivable, to scan
The million forms of God those stars unroll
When, in our turn, we show to them a Man.

Beyond Knowledge

'Your sins . . . shall be white as snow.'

INTO the rescued world newcomer,
    The newly-dead stepped up, and cried,
'Oh, what is that, sweeter than summer
    Was to my heart before I died?
Sir (to an angel), what is yonder
    More bright than the remembered skies,
A lovelier sight, a softer splendour
    Than when the moon was wont to rise?
Surely no sinner wears such seeming
    Even the Rescued World within?'

'Oh, the success of His redeeming!
    O child, it is a rescued sin!'

E

A Thrush before Dawn

A VOICE peals in this end of night
     A phrase of notes resembling stars,
Single and spiritual notes of light.
    What call they at my window-bars?
       The South, the past, the day to be,
       An ancient infelicity.

Darkling, deliberate, what sings
    This wonderful one, alone, at peace?
What wilder things than song, what things
    Sweeter than youth, clearer than Greece,
       Dearer than Italy, untold
       Delight, and freshness centuries old?

And first first-loves, a multitude,
    The exaltation of their pain;
Ancestral childhood long renewed;
    And midnights of invisible rain;
       And gardens, gardens, night and day,
       Gardens and childhood all the way.

What Middle Ages passionate,
    O passionate voice! What distant bells
Lodged in the hills, what palace state
    Illyrian! For it speaks, it tells,
       Without desire, without dismay,
       Some morrow and some yesterday.

66

All-natural things! But more—Whence came
   This yet remoter mystery?
How do these starry notes proclaim
   A graver still divinity?
      This hope, this sanctity of fear?

O innocent throat! O human ear!

Length of Days: to the early dead in battle

THERE is no length of days
But yours, boys who were children once. Of old
The Past beset you in your childish ways,
    With sense of Time untold.

    What have you then forgone?
A history? This you had. Or memories?
These, too, you had of your far-distant dawn.
    No further dawn seems his,

    The old man who shares with you,
But has no more, no more. Time's mystery
Did once for him the most that it can do:
    He has had infancy.

    And all his dreams, and all
His loves for mighty Nature, sweet and few,
Are but the dwindling past he can recall
    Of what his childhood knew.

    He counts not any more
His brief, his present years. But oh, he knows
How far apart the summers were of yore,
    How far apart the snows.

    Therefore be satisfied;
Long life is in your treasury ere you fall;
Yes, and first love, like Dante's. Oh, a bride
    For ever mystical!

    Irrevocable good,—
You dead, and now about, so young, to die,—
Your childhood was; there Space, there Multitude,
    There dwelt Antiquity.

Summer in England, 1914

ON London fell a clearer light;
   Caressing pencils of the sun
Defined the distances, the white
   Houses transfigured one by one,
The 'long, unlovely street' impearled.
Oh, what a sky has walked the world!

Most happy year! And out of town
   The hay was prosperous, and the wheat;
The silken harvest climbed the down:
   Moon after moon was heavenly-sweet,
Stroking the bread within the sheaves,
Looking 'twixt apples and their leaves.

And while this rose made round her cup,
   The armies died convulsed. And when
This chaste young silver sun went up
   Softly, a thousand shattered men,
One wet corruption, heaped the plain,
After a league-long throb of pain.

Flower following tender flower; and birds,
   And berries; and benignant skies
Made thrive the serried flocks and herds.—
   Yonder are men shot through the eyes.
     Love, hide thy face
From man's unpardonable race.

*   *   *

Who said 'No man hath greater love than this,
   To die to serve his friend'?
So these have loved us all unto the end.
   Chide thou no more, O thou unsacrificed!
The soldier dying dies upon a kiss,
   The very kiss of Christ.

A Wind of Clear Weather in England

O WHAT a miracle wind is this
   Has crossed the English land to-day
With an unprecedented kiss,
   And wonderfully found a way!

Unsmirched incredibly and clean,
   Between the towns and factories,
Avoiding, has his long flight been,
   Bringing a sky like Sicily's.

O fine escape, horizon pure
   As Rome's! Black chimneys left and right,
But not for him, the straight, the sure,
   His luminous day, his spacious night.

How keen his choice, how swift his feet!
   Narrow the way and hard to find!
This delicate stepper and discreet
   Walked not like any worldly wind.

Most like a man in man's own day,
   One of the few, a perfect one:
His open earth—the single way;
   His narrow road—the open sun.

To Olivia, *of her Dark Eyes*

ACROSS what calm of tropic seas,
 'Neath alien clusters of the nights,
Looked, in the past, such eyes as these?
 Long-quenched, relumed, ancestral lights!

The generations fostered them;
 And steadfast Nature, secretwise—
Thou seedling child of that old stem—
 Kindled anew thy dark-bright eyes.

Was it a century or two
 This lovely darkness rose and set,
Occluded by grey eyes and blue,
 And Nature feigning to forget?

Some grandam gave a hint of it—
 So cherished was it in thy race,
So fine a treasure to transmit
 In its perfection to thy face.

Some father to some mother's breast
 Entrusted it, unknowing. Time
Implied, or made it manifest,
 Bequest of a forgotten clime.

Hereditary eyes! But this
 Is single, singular, apart:—
New-made thy love, new-made thy kiss,
 New-made thy errand to my heart.

Free Will

D EAR are some hidden things
My soul has sealed in silence; past delights;
Hope unconfessed; desires with hampered wings,
Remembered in the nights.

But my best treasures are
Ignoble, undelightful, abject, cold;
Yet oh, profounder hoards oracular
No reliquaries hold.

There lie my trespasses,
Abjured but not disowned. I'll not accuse
Determinism, nor, as the Master* says,
Charge even 'the poor Deuce'.

Under my hand they lie,
My very own, my proved iniquities;
And though the glory of my life go by
I hold and garner these.

How else, how otherwhere,
How otherwise, shall I discern and grope
For lowliness? How hate, how love, how dare,
How weep, how hope?

* George Meredith.

73

In Sleep

I DREAMT (no 'dream' awake—a dream indeed)
A wrathful man was talking in the park:
'Where are the Higher Powers, who know our need
    And leave us in the dark?

'There are no Higher Powers; there is no heart
In God, no love'—his oratory here,
Taking the paupers' and the cripples' part,
    Was broken by a tear.

And then it seemed that One who did create
Compassion, who alone invented pity,
Walked, as though called, in at that north-east gate,
    Out from the muttering city;

Threaded the little crowd, trod the brown grass,
Bent o'er the speaker close, saw the tear rise,
And saw Himself, as one looks in a glass,
    In those impassioned eyes.

Easter Night

ALL night had shout of men and cry
　Of woeful women filled His way;
Until that noon of sombre sky
　　On Friday, clamour and display
Smote Him; no solitude had He,
No silence, since Gethsemane.

Public was Death; but Power, but Might,
　　But Life again, but Victory,
Were hushed within the dead of night,
　　The shutter'd dark, the secrecy.
And all alone, alone, alone,
He rose again behind the stone.

The Lord's Prayer

Audemus dicere 'Pater Noster': CANON OF THE MASS

THERE is a bolder way,
    There is a wilder enterprise than this
All-human iteration day by day.
Courage, mankind! Restore Him what is His.

Out of His mouth were given
These phrases. Oh, replace them whence they came.
He, only, knows our inconceivable 'Heaven',
Our hidden 'Father', and the unspoken 'Name';

Our 'trespasses', our 'bread',
The 'will' inexorable yet implored;
The miracle-words that are and are not said,
Charged with the unknown purpose of their Lord.

'Forgive', 'give', 'lead us not'—
Speak them by Him, O man the unaware,
Speak by that dear tongue, though thou know not what,
Shuddering through the paradox of prayer.

The Divine Privilege

LORD, where are Thy prerogatives?
  Why, men have more than Thou hast kept;
The king rewards, remits, forgives,
  The poet to a throne has stept.

And Thou, despoiled, hast given away
  Worship to men, success to strife,
Thy glory to the heavenly day,
  And made Thy sun the lord of life.

Is one too precious to impart,
  One property reserved to Christ,
One, cherished, grappled to that heart?
  —To be alone the Sacrificed?

O Thou who lovest to redeem!—
  One whom I know lies sore oppressed.
Thou wilt not suffer me to dream
  That I can bargain for her rest.

Seven hours I swiftly sleep, while she
  Measures the leagues of dark, awake.
Oh, that my dewy eyes might be
  Parched by a vigil for her sake!

But oh, rejected! Oh, in vain!
  I cannot give who would not keep.
I cannot buy, I cannot gain,
  I cannot give her half my sleep.

A Father of Women: AD SOROREM E. B.

'Thy father was transfused into thy blood.'
DRYDEN: *Ode to Mrs. Anne Killigrew.*

OUR father works in us,
The daughters of his manhood. Not undone
Is he, not wasted, though transmuted thus,
And though he left no son.

Therefore on him I cry
To arm me: 'For my delicate mind a casque,
A breastplate for my heart, courage to die,
Of thee, captain, I ask.

'Nor strengthen only; press
A finger on this violent blood and pale,
Over this rash will let thy tenderness
A while pause, and prevail.

'And shepherd-father, thou
Whose staff folded my thoughts before my birth,
Control them now I am of earth, and now
Thou art no more of earth.

'O liberal, constant, dear,
Crush in my nature the ungenerous art
Of the inferior; set me high, and here,
Here garner up thy heart!'

Like to him now are they,
The million living fathers of the War—
Mourning the crippled world, the bitter day—
Whose striplings are no more.

The crippled world! Come then,
Fathers of women with your honour in trust,
Approve, accept, know them daughters of men,
Now that your sons are dust.

Nurse Edith Cavell

Two o'clock, the morning of October 12th, 1915

To her accustomed eyes
  The midnight-morning brought not such a dread
As thrills the chance-awakened head that lies
In trivial sleep on the habitual bed.

   'Twas yet some hours ere light;
And many, many, many a break of day
Had she outwatched the dying; but this night
Shortened her vigil was, briefer the way.

   By dial of the clock
'Twas day in the dark above her lonely head.
'This day thou shalt be with Me.' Ere the cock
Announced that day she met the Immortal Dead.

To Tintoretto in Venice

*The Art of Painting had in the Primitive years looked with the
light, not towards it. Before Tintoretto's date, however, many
painters practised shadows and lights, and turned more or less
sunwards: but he set the figure between himself and a full sun.
His work is to be known in Venice by the splendid trick of an
occluded sun and a shadow thrown straight at the spectator.*

MASTER, thy enterprise,
　Magnificent, magnanimous, was well done,
Which seized the head of Art, and turned her eyes—
The simpleton—and made her front the sun.

　　Long had she sat content,
Her young unlessoned back to a morning gay,
To a solemn noon, to a cloudy firmament,
And looked upon a world in gentle day.

　　But thy imperial call
Bade her to stand with thee and breast the light,
And therefore face the shadows, mystical,
Sombre, translucent vestiges of night,

　　Yet glories of the day.
Eagle! we know thee by thy undaunted eyes
Sky-ward, and by thy glooms; we know thy way
Ambiguous, and those halo-misted dyes.

　　Thou Cloud, the bridegroom's friend
(The bridegroom sun)! Master, we know thy sign:
A mystery of hues world-without-end;
And hide-and-seek of gamesome and divine;

Shade of the noble head
Cast hitherward upon the noble breast;
Human solemnities thrice hallowèd;
The haste to Calvary, the Cross at rest.

Look sunward, Angel, then!
Carry the fortress-heavens by that hand;
Still be the interpreter of suns to men;
And shadow us, O thou Tower! for thou shalt stand.

OF BIRTH, 1864; OF DEATH, 1916

TO SHAKESPEARE

Longer than thine, than thine,
  Is now my time of life; and thus thy years
Seem to be clasped and harboured within mine.
Oh, how ignoble this my clasp appears!

    Thy unprophetic birth,
Thy darkling death: living I might have seen
That cradle, marked those labours, closed that earth.
O first, O last, O infinite between!

    Now that my life has shared
Thy dedicated date, O mortal, twice,
To what all-vain embrace shall be compared
My lean enclosure of thy paradise:

    To ignorant arms that fold
A poet to a foolish breast? The Line,
That is not, with the world within its hold?
So, days with days, my days encompass thine.

    Child, Stripling, Man—the sod.
Might I talk little language to thee, pore
On thy last silence? O thou city of God,
My waste lies after thee, and lies before.

The Treasure

THREE times have I beheld
Fear leap in a babe's face, and take his breath,
Fear, like the fear of eld
That knows the price of life, the name of death.

What is it justifies
This thing, this dread, this fright that has no tongue,
The terror in those eyes
When only eyes can speak—they are so young?

Not yet those eyes had wept.
What does fear cherish that it locks so well?
What fortress is thus kept?
Of what is ignorant terror sentinel?

And pain in the poor child,
Monstrously disproportionate, and dumb
In the poor beast, and wild
In the old decorous man, caught, overcome?

Of what the outposts these?
Of what the fighting guardians? What demands
That sense of menaces,
And then such flying feet, imploring hands?

Life: There's nought else to seek;
Life only, little prized; but by design
Of nature prized. How weak,
How sad, how brief! Oh, how divine, divine!

'A RIDDLING world!' one cried.
  'If pangs must be, would God that they were sent
To the impure, the cruel, and passed aside
    The holy innocent!'

    But I, 'Ah no, no, no!
Not the clean heart transpierced; not tears that fall
For a child's agony; nor a martyr's woe;
    Not these, not these appal.

    'Not docile motherhood,
Dutiful, frequent, closed in all distress;
Not shedding of the unoffending blood;
    Not little joy grown less;

    'Not all-benign old age
With dotage mocked; not gallantry that faints
And still pursues; not the vile heritage
    Of sin's disease in saints;

    'Not these defeat the mind.
For great is that abjection, and august
That irony. Submissive we shall find
    A splendour in that dust.

    'Not these puzzle the will;
Not these the yet unanswered question urge.
But the unjust stricken; but the hands that kill
    Lopped; but the merited scourge;

    'The sensualist at fast;
The merciless felled; the liar in his snares.
The cowardice of my judgement sees, aghast,
    The flail, the chaff, the tares.'

The Poet and his Book

Here are my thoughts, alive within this fold,
My simple sheep. Their shepherd, I grow wise
As dearly, gravely, deeply I behold
        Their different eyes.

O distant pastures in their blood! O streams
  From watersheds that fed them for this prison!
Lights from aloft, midsummer suns in dreams,
        Set and arisen.

They wander out, but all return anew,
  The small ones, to this heart to which they clung;
'And those that are with young,' the fruitful few
        That are with young.

Intimations of Mortality from recollections
of early childhood

A simple child . . .
    That lightly draws its breath
And feels its life in every limb,
    What should it know of death?
                                    Wordsworth

IT knows but will not tell.
    Awake, alone, it counts its father's years—
How few are left—its mother's. Ah, how well
    It knows of death, in tears.

If any of the three—
    Parents and child—believe they have prevailed
To keep the secret of mortality,
    I know that two have failed.

The third, the lonely, keeps
    One secret—a child's knowledge. When they come
At night to ask wherefore the sweet one weeps,
    Those hidden lips are dumb.

The Wind is Blind

'*Eyeless, in Gaza, at the mill, with slaves.*'
MILTON'S *Samson*

THE wind is blind.
The earth sees sun and moon; the height
  Is watch-tower to the dawn; the plain
Shines to the summer; visible light
  Is scattered in the drops of rain.

  The wind is blind.
The flashing billows are aware;
  With open eyes the cities see;
Light leaves the ether, everywhere
  Known to the homing bird and bee.

  The wind is blind,
Is blind alone. How has he hurled
  His ignorant lash, his aimless dart,
His eyeless rush, upon the world,
  Unseeing, to break his unknown heart!

  The wind is blind,
And the sail traps him, and the mill
  Captures him; and he cannot save
His swiftness and his desperate will
  From those blind uses of the slave.

To his devoted heart*
  Who, young, had loved his ageing mate for life,
In late lone years Time gave the elder's part,
  Time gave the bridegroom's boast, Time gave a
    younger wife.

A wilder prank and plot
  Time soon will promise, threaten, offering me
Impossible things that Nature suffers not—
  A daughter's riper mind, a child's seniority.

Oh, by my filial tears
  Mourned all too young, Father! on this my head
Time yet will force at last the longer years,
  Claiming some strange respect for me from you, the
    dead.

Nay, nay! Too new to know
  Time's conjuring is, too great to understand.
Memory has not died; it leaves me so—
  Leaning a fading brow on your unfaded hand.

   *Dr. Johnson outlived by thirty years his wife, who was
twenty years his senior.

The Threshing-Machine

No 'fan is in his hand' for these
Young villagers beneath the trees,
    Watching the wheels. But I recall
The rhythm of rods that rise and fall,
Purging the harvest, over-seas.

No fan, no flail, no threshing-floor!
And all their symbols evermore
    Forgone in England now—the sign,
    The visible pledge, the threat divine,
The chaff dispersed, the wheat in store.

The unbreathing engine marks no tune,
Steady at sunrise, steady at noon,
    Inhuman, perfect, saving time,
    And saving measure, and saving rhyme—
And did our Ruskin speak too soon?

'No noble strength on earth' he sees
'Save Hercules' arm'. His grave decrees
    Curse wheel and steam. As the wheels ran
    I saw the other strength of man,
I knew the brain of Hercules.

Winter Trees on the Horizon

O DELICATE! Even in wooded lands
     They show the margin of my world,
My own horizon; little bands
     Of twigs unveil that edge impearled,

And what is more mine own than this—
     My limit, level with mine eyes?
For me precisely do they kiss—
     The rounded earth, the rounding skies.

It has my stature, that keen line
     (Let mathematics vouch for it).
The lark's horizon is not mine,
     No, nor his nestlings' where they sit;

No, nor the child's. And, when I gain
     The hills, I lift it as I rise
Erect; anon, back to the plain
     I soothe it with mine equal eyes.

To Sleep

Dear fool, be true to me!
 I know the poets speak thee fair, and I
Hail thee uncivilly.
Oh, but I call with a more urgent cry!

I do not prize thee less,
I need thee more, that thou dost love to teach—
 Father of foolishness—
The imbecile dreams clear out of wisdom's reach.

Come and release me; bring
My irresponsible mind; come in thy hours;
 Draw from my soul the sting
Of wit that trembles, consciousness that cowers.

For if night comes without thee
She is more cruel than day. But thou, fulfil
 Thy work, thy gifts about thee—
Liberty, liberty, from this weight of will.

My day-mind can endure
Upright, in hope, all it must undergo.
 But oh, afraid, unsure,
My night-mind waking lies too low, too low.

Dear fool, be true to me!
The night is thine, man yields it, it beseems
 Thy ironic dignity.
Make me all night the innocent fool that dreams.

'The Marriage of True Minds'

In the Bach-Gounod 'Ave Maria'

THAT seeking Prelude found its unforetold
    Unguessed intention, trend;
Though needing no fulfilment, did enfold
    This exquisite end.

Bach led his notes up through their delicate slope
    Aspiring, so they sound,
And so they were, in some strange ignorant hope
    Thus to be crowned.

What deep soft seas beneath this buoyant barque!
    What winds to speed this bird!
What impulses to toss this heavenward lark!
    Thought—then the word.

Lovely the tune, lovely the unconsciousness
    Of him who promised it.
Lovely the years that joined in blessedness
    The two, the fit.

Bach was Precursor. But no Baptist's cry
    Was his; he, who began
For one who was to end, did prophesy,
    By Nature's generous act, the lesser man.

In Honour of America, 1917

In antithesis to Rossetti's 'On the Refusal of Aid between Nations'

Not that the earth is changing, O my God!
Not that her brave democracies take heart
To share, to rule her treasure, to impart
The wine to those who long the wine-press trod;
Not therefore trust we that beneath Thy nod,
Thy silent benediction, even now
In gratitude so many nations bow,
So many poor: not therefore, O my God!

But because living men for dying man
Go to a million deaths, to deal one blow;
And justice speaks one great compassionate tongue;
And nation unto nation calls 'One clan
We succourers are, one tribe!' By this we know
Our earth holds confident, steadfast, being young.

'Lord, I owe Thee a Death' : RICHARD HOOKER

IN TIME OF WAR

MAN pays that debt with new munificence,
Not piecemeal now, not slowly, by the old:
Not grudgingly, by the effaced thin pence,
But greatly and in gold.

Reflexions

1 *In Ireland*

A MIRROR faced a mirror: ire and hate
Opposite ire and hate; the multiplied,
The complex charge rejected, intricate,
   From side to sullen side;

One plot, one crime, one treachery, nay, one name,
   Assumed, denounced, in echoes of replies.
The doubt, exchanged, lit thousands of one flame
   Within those mutual eyes.

2 *In 'Othello'*

A MIRROR faced a mirror: in sweet pain
His dangers with her pity did she track,
Received her pity with his love again,
   And these she wafted back.

That masculine passion in her little breast
   She bandied with him; her compassion he
Bandied with her. What tender sport! No rest
   Had love's infinity.

3 *In Two Poets*

A MIRROR faced a mirror: O thy word,
Thou lord of images, did lodge in me,
Locked to my heart, homing from home, a bird,
   A carrier, bound for thee.

Thy migratory greatness, greater far
   For that return, returns; now grow divine
By endlessness my visiting thoughts, that are
   Those visiting thoughts of thine.

To Conscripts

Compel them to come in: ST. LUKE'S GOSPEL

Y ou 'made a virtue of necessity'
   By divine sanction; you, the loth, the grey,
The random, gentle, unconvinced; oh, be
   The crowned!—you may, you may.

You, the compelled, be feasted! You, the caught,
   Be freemen of the gates that word unlocks!
Accept your victory from that unsought,
   That heavenly, paradox.

G

The Voice of a Bird

He shall rise up at the voice of a bird: ECCLESIASTES

WHO then is 'he'?
   Dante, Keats, Shakespeare, Milton, Shelley; all
Rose in their greatness at the shrill decree,
The little rousing inarticulate call.

   For they stood up
At the bird-voice, of lark, of nightingale,
Drank poems from that throat as from a cup.
Over the great world's notes did these prevail.

   And not alone
The signal poets woke. In listening man,
Woman, and child a poet stirs unknown,
Throughout the Mays of birds since Mays began.

   He rose, he heard—
Our father, our St. Peter, in his tears—
The crowing, twice, of the prophetic bird,
The saddest cock-crow of our human years.

The Laws of Verse

DEAR laws, come to my breast!
Take all my frame, and make your close arms meet
Around me; and so ruled, so warmed, so pressed,
I breathe, aware; I feel my wild heart beat.

Dear laws, be wings to me!
The feather merely floats. Oh, be it heard
Through weight of life—the skylark's gravity—
That I am not a feather, but a bird.

The Question

Il poeta mi disse, 'Che pensi?': DANTE

VIRGIL stayed Dante with a wayside word;
    But long, and low, and loud, and urgently,
The poets of my passion have I heard
        Summoning me.

It is their closest whisper and their call.
Their greatness to this lowliness hath spoken,
Their voices rest upon that interval,
        Their sign, their token.

Man at his little prayer tells Heaven his thought,
To man entrusts his thought—'Friend, this is mine.'
The immortal poets within my breast have sought,
        Saying, 'What is thine?'

'The Return to Nature' in Poetry

1 Prometheus

IT was the south: mid-everything,
    Mid-land, mid-summer, noon;
And deep within a limpid spring
    The mirrored sun of June.

Splendour in freshness! Ah, who stole
    This sun, this fire, from heaven?
He holds it shining in his soul,
    Prometheus the forgiven.

2 Thetis

IN her bright title poets dare
    What the wild eye of fancy sees—
Similitude—the clear, the fair
    Light mystery of images.

Round the blue sea I love the best
    The argent foam played, slender, fleet;
I saw—past Wordsworth and the rest—
    Her natural, Greek, and silver feet.

To Silence

*'Space, the bound of a solid': Silence, then, the
form of a melody*

Not, Silence, for thine idleness I raise
My silence-bounded singing in thy praise,
But for thy moulding of my Mozart's tune,
Thy hold upon the bird that sings the moon,
      Thy magisterial ways.

Man's lovely definite melody-shapes are thine,
Outlined, controlled, compressed, complete, divine.
Also thy fine intrusions do I trace,
Thy afterthoughts, thy wandering, thy grace,
      Within the poet's line.

Thy secret is the song that is to be.
Music had never stature but for thee,
Sculptor! strong as the sculptor Space whose hand
Urged the Discobolus and bade him stand.
    *   *   *   *   *   *
Man, on his way to Silence, stops to hear and see.

The English Metres

THE rooted liberty of flowers in breeze
  Is theirs, by national luck impulsive, terse,
Tethered, uncaptured, rules obeyed 'at ease',
  Time-strengthened laws of verse.

Or they are like our seasons that admit
  Inflexion, not infraction: Autumn hoar,
Winter more tender than our thoughts of it,
  But a year's steadfast four;

Redundant syllables of Summer rain,
  And displaced accents of authentic Spring;
Spondaic clouds above a gusty plain
  With dactyls on the wing.

Not Common Law, but Equity, is theirs—
  Our metres; play and agile foot askance,
And distant, beckoning, blithely rhyming pairs,
  Unknown to classic France;

Unknown to Italy. Ay, count, collate,
  Latins! with eye foreseeing on the time,
And numbered fingers, and approaching fate
  On the appropriate rhyme.

Nay, nobly our grave measures are decreed:
  Heroic, Alexandrine with the stay,
Deliberate; or else like him whose speed
  Did outrun Peter, urgent in the break of day.

'Rivers unknown to Song' : JAMES THOMSON

WIDE waters in the waste; or, out of reach,
　　Rough Alpine falls where late a glacier hung;
Or rivers groping for the alien beach,
　　Through continents, unsung.

Nay, not these nameless, these remote, alone;
　　But all the streams from all the watersheds—
Peneus, Danube, Nile—are the unknown
　　Young in their ancient beds.

Man has no tale for them. O travellers swift
　　From secrets to oblivion! Waters wild
That pass in act to bend a flower, or lift
　　The bright limbs of a child!

For they are new, they are fresh; there's no surprise
　　Like theirs on earth. O strange for evermore!
This moment's Tiber with his shining eyes
　　Never saw Rome before.

Man has no word for their eternity—
　　Rhine, Avon, Arno, younglings, youth uncrowned:
Ignorant, innocent, instantaneous, free,
　　Unwelcomed, unrenowned.

To the Mother of Christ the Son of Man

WE too (one cried), we too,
  We the unready, the perplexed, the cold,
Must shape the Eternal in our thoughts anew,
  Cherish, possess, enfold.

  Thou sweetly, we in strife.
It is our passion to conceive Him thus
In mind, in sense, within our house of life;
  That seed is locked in us.

  We must affirm our Son
From the ambiguous Nature's difficult speech,
Gather in darkness that resplendent One,
  Close as our grasp can reach.

  Nor shall we ever rest
From this our task. An hour sufficed for thee,
Thou innocent! He lingers in the breast
  Of our humanity.

A Comparison in a Seaside Field

'Tis royal and authentic June
　　Over this poor soil blossoming
Here lies, beneath an upright noon,
　　Thin nation for so wild a king.

Far off, the noble Summer rules,
　　Violent in the ardent rose,
His sun alight in mirroring pools,
　　Braggart on Alps of vanquished snows;

Away, aloft, true to his hour,
　　Announced, his colour, his fire, his jest.
But here, in negligible flower,
　　Summer is not proclaimed:—confessed.

A woman I marked; for her no state,
　　Small joy, no song. She had her boon,
Her only youth, true to its date,
　　Faintly perceptible, her June.

Surmise

Not wish, nor fear, nor quite expectancy
Is that vague spirit Surmise,
That wanderer, that wonderer, whom we see
  Within each other's eyes;

And yet not often. For she flits away,
  Fitful as infant thought,
Visitant at a venture, hope at play,
  Unversed in facts, untaught.

In 'the wide fields of possibility'
  Surmise, conjecturing,
Makes little trials, incredulous, that flee
  Abroad on random wing.

One day this inarticulate shall find speech,
  This hoverer seize our breath.
Surmise shall close with man—with all, with each—
  In her own sovereign hour, the moments of our death.

To Antiquity

'Reverence for our fathers, with their stores of experiences' :
An author whose name I did not note

O OUR young ancestor,
Our boy in Letters, how we trudge oppressed
With our 'experiences,' and you of yore
    Flew light, and blessed!

Youngling, in your new town,
    Tight, like a box of toys—the town that is
Our shattered, open ruin, with its crown
    Of histories;

You with your morning words
    Fresh from the night, your yet un-sonneted moon;
Your passion undismayed, cool as a bird's
    Ignorant tune;

O youngling! how is this?
    Your poems are not wearied yet, not dead.
Must I bow low? or, with an envious kiss,
    Put you to bed?

Christmas Night

'If I cannot see Thee present I will mourn Thee absent,
for this also is a proof of love': THOMAS À KEMPIS

WE do not find Him on the difficult earth,
   In surging humankind,
In wayside death or accidental birth,
   Or in the 'march of mind'.

Nature, her nests, her prey, the fed, the caught
   Hide Him so well, so well,
His steadfast secret there seems to our thought
   Life's saddest miracle.

He's but conjectured in man's happiness,
   Suspected in man's tears,
Or lurks beyond the long, discouraged guess,
   Grown fainter through the years.

   *   *   *   *   *   *

But absent, absent now? Ah, what is this,
   Near as in child-birth bed,
Laid on our sorrowful hearts, close to a kiss?
   A homeless childish head.

Autumn is weary, halt, and old;
  Ah, but she owns the song of joy!
Her colours fade, her woods are cold:
  Her singing-bird's a boy, a boy.

In lovely Spring the birds were bent
  On nests, on use, on love, forsooth!
Grown-up were they. This boy's content,
  For his is liberty, his is youth.

The musical stripling sings for play
  Taking no thought, and virgin-glad.
For duty sang those mates in May.
  This singing-bird's a lad, a lad.

To 'A Certain Rich Man'

'I have five brethren. . . . Father, I beseech Thee . . . lest they come to this place'

THOU wouldst not part thy spoil
  Gained from the beggar's want, the weakling's toil,
Nor spare a jot of sumptuousness or state
For Lazarus at the gate.

And in the appalling night
Of expiation, as in day's delight,
Thou heldst thy niggard hand; it would not share
One hour of thy despair.

Those five—thy prayer for them!
O generous! who, condemned, wouldst not condemn,
Whose ultimate human greatness proved thee so
A miser of thy woe.

'Everlasting farewells! and again and yet again
. . . everlasting farewells!' : DE QUINCEY

'FAREWELLS!' oh, what a word!
   Denying this agony, denying the affrights,
Denying all De Quincey spoke or heard
In the infernal sadness of his nights.

How mend these strange 'farewells'?
'Vale'? 'Addio'? 'Leb' wohl'? Not one but seems
A tranquil refutation; tolling bells
That yet withhold the terror of his dreams.

The Poet to the Birds

You bid me hold my peace,
    Or so I think, you birds; you'll not forgive
My kill-joy song that makes the wild song cease,
    Silent or fugitive.

Yon thrush stopt in mid-phrase
    At my mere footfall; and a longer note
Took wing and fled afield, and went its ways
    Within the blackbird's throat.

Hereditary song,
    Illyrian lark and Paduan nightingale,
Is yours, unchangeable the ages long;
    Assyria heard your tale;

Therefore you do not die.
    But single, local, lonely, mortal, new,
Unlike, and thus like all my race, am I,
    Preluding my adieu.

My human song must be
    My human thought. Be patient till 'tis done.
I shall not hold my little peace; for me
    There is no peace but one.

EARLY POEMS

first printed in *Preludes*, 1875, and chosen by the Author
for reprinting in *Collected Poems*, 1913.

In Early Spring

O SPRING, I know thee! Seek for sweet surprise
    In the young children's eyes.
But I have learnt the years, and know the yet
    Leaf-folded violet.
Mine ear, awake to silence, can foretell
    The cuckoo's fitful bell.
I wander in a grey time that encloses
    June and the wild hedge-roses.
A year's procession of the flowers doth pass
    My feet, along the grass.
And all you wild birds silent yet, I know
    The notes that stir you so,
Your songs yet half devised in the dim dear
    Beginnings of the year.
In these young days you meditate your part;
    I have it all by heart.
I know the secrets of the seeds of flowers
    Hidden and warm with showers,
And how, in kindling Spring, the cuckoo shall
    Alter his interval.
But not a flower or song I ponder is
    My own, but memory's.
I shall be silent in those days desired
    Before a world inspired.

O all brown birds, compose your old song-phrases,
      Earth, thy familiar daisies!

A poet mused upon the dusky height,
      Between two stars towards night,
His purpose in his heart. I watched, a space,
      The meaning of his face:
There was the secret, fled from earth and skies,
      Hid in his grey young eyes.
My heart and all the Summer wait his choice,
      And wonder for his voice.
Who shall foretell his songs, and who aspire
      But to divine his lyre?
Sweet earth, we know thy dimmest mysteries,
      But he is lord of his.

Parted

FAREWELL to one now silenced quite,
Sent out of hearing, out of sight,—
　My friend of friends, whom I shall miss.
　He is not banished, though, for this,—
Nor he, nor sadness, nor delight.

Though I shall talk with him no more,
A low voice sounds upon the shore.
　He must not watch my resting-place,
　But who shall drive a mournful face
From the sad winds about my door?

I shall not hear his voice complain,
But who shall stop the patient rain?
　His tears must not disturb my heart,
　But who shall change the years, and part
The world from every thought of pain?

Although my life is left so dim
The morning crowns the mountain-rim,
　Joy is not gone from summer skies,
　Nor innocence from children's eyes;
And all these things are part of him.

He is not banished, for the showers
Yet wake this green warm earth of ours.
　How can the summer but be sweet?
　I shall not have him at my feet,
And yet my feet are on the flowers.

To any Poet

THOU who singest through the earth
    All the earth's wild creatures fly thee;
Everywhere thou marrest mirth—
    Dumbly they defy thee;
There is something they deny thee.

Pines thy fallen nature ever
For the unfallen Nature sweet.
But she shuns thy long endeavour,
    Though her flowers and wheat
Throng and press thy pausing feet.

Though thou tame a bird to love thee,
Press thy face to grass and flowers,
All these things reserve above thee
    Secrets in the bowers,
Secrets in the sun and showers.

Sing thy sorrow, sing thy gladness,
In thy songs must wind and tree
Bear the fictions of thy sadness,
    Thy humanity.
For their truth is not for thee.

Wait, and many a secret nest,
Many a hoarded winter-store
Will be hidden on thy breast.
    Things thou longest for
Will not fear or shun thee more.

Thou shalt intimately lie
In the roots of flowers that thrust
Upwards from thee to the sky,
    With no more distrust
When they blossom from thy dust.

Silent labours of the rain
Shall be near thee, reconciled;
Little lives of leaves and grain,
   All things shy and wild,
Tell thee secrets, quiet child.

Earth, set free from thy fair fancies
And the art thou shalt resign,
Will bring forth her rue and pansies
   Unto more divine
Thoughts than any thoughts of thine.

Nought will fear thee, humbled creature.
There will lie thy mortal burden
Pressed unto the heart of Nature,
   Songless in a garden,
With a long embrace of pardon.

Then the truth all creatures tell,
And His will Whom thou entreatest
Shall absorb thee; there shall dwell
   Silence, the completest
Of thy poems, last and sweetest.

The Spring to the Summer

The Poet sings to her Poet

O POET of the time to be,
My conqueror, I began for thee.
    Enter into thy poet's pain,
    And take the riches of the rain,
And make the perfect year for me.

Thou unto whom my lyre shall fall,
Whene'er thou comest, hear my call.
    Oh, keep the promise of my lays,
    Take thou the parable of my days;
I trust thee with the aim of all.

And if thy thoughts unfold from me,
Know that I too have hints of thee,
    Dim hopes that come across my mind
    In the rare days of warmer wind,
And tones of summer in the sea.

And I have set thy paths, I guide
Thy blossoms on the wild hillside.
    And I, thy bygone poet, share
    The flowers that throng thy feet where'er
I led thy feet before I died.

To the Beloved

AH, not more subtly silence strays
    Amongst the winds, between the voices,
Mingling alike with pensive lays,
    And with the music that rejoices,
Than thou art present in my days.

My silence, life returns to thee
    In all the pauses of her breath.
Hush back to rest the melody
    That out of thee awakeneth;
And thou, wake ever, wake for me!

Thou art like silence all unvexed,
    Though wild words part my soul from thee.
Thou art like silence unperplexed,
    A secret and a mystery
Between one footfall and the next.

Most dear pause in a mellow lay!
    Thou art inwoven with every air.
With thee the wildest tempests play,
    And snatches of thee everywhere
Make little heavens throughout a day.

Darkness and solitude shine, for me.
    For life's fair outward part are rife
The silver noises; let them be.
    It is the very soul of life
Listens for thee, listens for thee.

O pause between the sobs of cares;
    O thought within all thought that is;
Trance between laughters unawares:
    Thou art the shape of melodies,
And thou the ecstasy of prayers.

Advent Meditation

Rorate cœli desuper, et nubes pluant Justum.
Aperiatur terra, et germinet Salvatorem.

No sudden thing of glory and fear
   Was the Lord's coming; but the dear
   Slow Nature's days followed each other
   To form the Saviour from His Mother
—One of the children of the year.

The earth, the rain, received the trust,
—The sun and dews, to frame the Just.
   He drew His daily life from these,
   According to His own decrees
Who makes man from the fertile dust.

Sweet summer and the winter wild,
These brought him forth, the Undefiled.
   The happy Springs renewed again
   His daily bread, the growing grain,
The food and raiment of the Child.

Your own fair Youth

Your own fair youth, you care so little for it—
  Smiling towards Heaven, you would not stay the
    advances
  Of time and change upon your happiest fancies.
I keep your golden hour, and will restore it.
If ever, in time to come, you would explore it—
  Your old self, whose thoughts went like last year's
    pansies—
  Look unto me; no mirror keeps its glances;
In my unfailing praises now I store it.

To guard all joys of yours from Time's estranging,
  I shall be then a treasury where your gay,
    Happy, and pensive past unaltered is.
I shall be then a garden charmed from changing,
  In which your June has never passed away.
    Walk there awhile among my memories.

In Autumn

THE leaves are many under my feet,
     And drift one way.
Their scent of death is weary and sweet.
     A flight of them is in the grey
Where sky and forest meet.

The low winds moan for dead sweet years;
     The birds sing all for pain,
Of a common thing, to weary ears,—
     Only a summer's fate of rain,
And a woman's fate of tears.

I walk to love and life alone
     Over these mournful places,
Across the summer overthrown,
     The dead joys of these silent faces,
To claim my own.

I know his heart has beat to bright
     Sweet loves gone by;
I know the leaves that die to-night
     Once budded to the sky;
And I shall die from his delight.

O leaves, so quietly ending now,
     You heard the cuckoos sing.
And I will grow upon my bough
     If only for a Spring,
And fall when the rain is on my brow.

O tell me, tell me ere you die,
    Is it worth the pain?
You bloomed so fair, you waved so high;
    Now that the sad days wane,
Are you repenting where you lie?

I lie amongst you, and I kiss
    Your fragrance mouldering.
O dead delights, is it such bliss,
    That tuneful Spring?
Is love so sweet, that comes to this?

Kiss me again as I kiss you;
    Kiss me again,
For all your tuneful nights of dew,
    In this your time of rain,
For all your kisses when Spring was new.

You will not, broken hearts; let be.
    I pass across your death
To a golden summer you shall not see,
    And in your dying breath
There is no benison for me.

There is an autumn yet to wane,
    There are leaves yet to fall,
Which, when I kiss, may kiss again,
    And, pitied, pity me all for all,
And love me in mist and rain.

A Letter from a Girl to her own Old Age

Listen, and when thy hand this paper presses,
  O time-worn woman, think of her who blesses
What thy thin fingers touch, with her caresses.

O mother, for the weight of years that break thee!
O daughter, for slow time must yet awake thee,
And from the changes of my heart must make thee!

O fainting traveller, morn is grey in heaven.
Dost thou remember how the clouds were driven?
And are they calm about the fall of even?

Pause near the ending of thy long migration,
For this one sudden hour of desolation
Appeals to one hour of thy meditation.

Suffer, O silent one, that I remind thee
Of the great hills that stormed the sky behind thee,
Of the wild winds of power that have resigned thee.

Know that the mournful plain where thou must wander
Is but a grey and silent world, but ponder
The misty mountains of the morning yonder.

Listen:—the mountain winds with rain were fretting,
And sudden gleams the mountain-tops besetting.
I cannot let thee fade to death, forgetting.

What part of this wild heart of mine I know not
Will follow with thee where the great winds blow not,
And where the young flowers of the mountain grow not.

Yet let my letter with my lost thoughts in it
Tell what the way was when thou didst begin it,
And win with thee the goal when thou shalt win it.

Oh, in some hour of thine my thoughts shall guide thee.
Suddenly, though time, darkness, silence, hide thee,
This wind from thy lost country flits beside thee,—

Telling thee: all thy memories moved the maiden,
With thy regrets was morning over-shaden,
With sorrow, thou hast left, her life was laden.

But whither shall my thoughts turn to pursue thee?
Life changes, and the years and days renew thee.
Oh, Nature brings my straying heart unto thee.

Her winds will join us, with their constant kisses
Upon the evening as the morning tresses,
Her summers breathe the same unchanging blisses.

And we, so altered in our shifting phases,
Track one another 'mid the many mazes
By the eternal child-breath of the daisies.

I have not writ this letter of divining
To make a glory of thy silent pining,
A triumph of thy mute and strange declining.

Only one youth, and the bright life was shrouded.
Only one morning, and the day was clouded.
And one old age with all regrets is crowded.

Oh, hush, Oh, hush! Thy tears my words are steeping.
Oh, hush, hush, hush! So full, the fount of weeping?
Poor eyes, so quickly moved, so near to sleeping?

Pardon the girl; such strange desires beset her.
Poor woman, lay aside the mournful letter
That breaks thy heart; the one who wrote, forget her:

The one who now thy faded features guesses,
With filial fingers thy grey hair caresses,
With morning tears thy mournful twilight blesses.

The Visiting Sea

As the inhastening tide doth roll,
  Home from the deep, along the whole
  Wide shining strand, and floods the caves,
    —Your love comes filling with happy waves
The open sea-shore of my soul.

But inland from the seaward spaces,
None knows, not even you, the places
  Brimmed, at your coming, out of sight,
    —The little solitudes of delight
This tide constrains in dim embraces.

You see the happy shore, wave-rimmed,
But know not of the quiet dimmed
  Rivers your coming floods and fills,
  The little pools 'mid happier hills,
My silent rivulets, over-brimmed.

What! I have secrets from you? Yes.
But, visiting Sea, your love doth press
  And reach in further than you know,
  And fills all these; and, when you go,
There's loneliness in loneliness.

Builders of Ruins

WE build with strength the deep tower wall
 That shall be shattered thus and thus.
And fair and great are court and hall,
 But *how* fair—this is not for us,
Who know the lack that lurks in all.

We know, we know how all too bright
 The hues are that our painting wears,
And how the marble gleams too white;—
 We speak in unknown tongues, the years
Interpret everything aright,

And crown with weeds our pride of towers,
 And warm our marble through with sun,
And break our pavements through with flowers,
 With an Amen when all is done,
Knowing these perfect things of ours.

O days, we ponder, left alone,
 Like children in their lonely hour,
And in our secrets keep your own,
 As seeds the colour of the flower.
To-day they are not all unknown,

The stars that 'twixt the rise and fall,
 Like relic-seers, shall one by one
Stand musing o'er our empty hall;
 And setting moons shall brood upon
The frescoes of our inward wall.

I

And when some midsummer shall be,
  Hither will come some little one
(Dusty with bloom of flowers is he),
  Sit on a ruin i' the late long sun,
And think, one foot upon his knee.

And where they wrought, these lives of ours,
  So many-worded, many-souled,
A North-West wind will take the towers,
  And dark with colour, sunny and cold,
Will range alone among the flowers.

And here or there, at our desire,
  The little clamorous owl shall sit
Through her still time; and we aspire
  To make a law (and know not it)
Unto the life of a wild briar.

Our purpose is distinct and dear,
  Though from our open eyes 'tis hidden.
Thou, Time to come, shalt make it clear,
  Undoing our work; we are children chidden
With pity and smiles of many a year.

Who shall allot the praise, and guess
  What part is yours and what is ours?—
O years that certainly will bless
  Our flowers with fruits, our seeds with flowers,
With ruin all our perfectness.

Be patient, Time, of our delays,
    Too happy hopes, and wasted fears,
Our faithful ways, our wilful ways;
    Solace our labours, O our seers
The seasons, and our bards the days;

And make our pause and silence brim
    With the shrill children's play, and sweets
Of those pathetic flowers and dim,
    Of those eternal flowers my Keats,
Dying, felt growing over him!

A Shattered Lute

I TOUCHED the heart that loved me as a player
Touches a lyre. Content with my poor skill,
   No touch save mine knew my beloved (and still
I thought at times: Is there no sweet lost air
Old loves could wake in him, I cannot share?).
   Oh, he alone, alone could so fulfil
   My thoughts in sound to the measure of my will.
He is gone, and silence takes me unaware.

The songs I knew not he resumes, set free
From my constraining love, alas for me!
   His part in our tune goes with him; my part
Is locked in me for ever; I stand as mute
   As one with vigorous music in his heart
Whose fingers stray upon a shattered lute.

The Day to the Night

The Poet sings to his Poet

FROM dawn to dusk, and from dusk to dawn,
We two are sundered always, Sweet.
A few stars shake o'er the rocky lawn
   And the cold sea-shore when we meet.
   The twilight comes with thy shadowy feet.

We are not day and night, my Fair,
   But one. It is an hour of hours.
And thoughts that are not otherwhere
   Are thought here 'mid the blown sea-flowers,
   This meeting and this dusk of ours.

Delight has taken Pain to her heart,
   And there is dusk and stars for these.
Oh, linger, linger! They would not part;
   And the wild wind comes from over-seas,
   With a new song to the olive trees.

And when we meet by the sounding pine
   Sleep draws near to his dreamless brother.
And when thy sweet eyes answer mine,
   Peace nestles close to her mournful mother,
   And Hope and Weariness kiss each other.

'Sœur Monique'

A Rondeau by Couperin

QUIET form of silent nun,
　　What has given you to my inward eyes?
What has marked you, unknown one,
In the throngs of centuries
That mine ears do listen through?
This old master's melody
That expresses you;
This admired simplicity,
Tender, with a serious wit;
And two words, the name of it,
　　'Sœur Monique.'

And if sad the music is,
It is sad with mysteries
Of a small immortal thing
That the passing ages sing,—
Simple music making mirth
Of the dying and the birth
Of the people of the earth.

No, not sad; we are beguiled,
Sad with living as we are;
Ours the sorrow, outpouring
Sad self on a selfless thing,
As our eyes and hearts are mild
With our sympathy for Spring,
With a pity sweet and wild
For the innocent and far,
With our sadness in a star,
Or our sadness in a child.

But two words, and this sweet air.
    Sœur Monique,
Had he more, who set you there?
Was his music-dream of you
Of some perfect nun he knew,
Or of some ideal, as true?

And I see you where you stand
With your life held in your hand
As a rosary of days.
And your thoughts in calm arrays,
And your innocent prayers are told
On your rosary of days.
And the young days and the old
With their quiet prayers did meet
When the chaplet was complete.

Did it vex you, the surmise
Of this wind of words, this storm of cries,
   Though you kept the silence so
   In the storms of long ago,
   And you keep it, like a star?
   —Of the evils triumphing,
Strong, for all your perfect conquering,
   Silenced conqueror that you are?

And I wonder at your peace, I wonder.
Would it trouble you to know,
Tender soul, the world and sin
By your calm feet trodden under
    Long ago,
Living now, mighty to win?
And your feet are vanished like the snow.
Vanished; but the poet, he

In whose dream your face appears,
He who ranges unknown years
With your music in his heart,
Speaks to you familiarly
Where you keep apart,
And invents you as you were.
And your picture, O my nun!
Is a strangely easy one,
For the holy weed you wear,
For your hidden eyes and hidden hair,
And in picturing you I may
Scarcely go astray.

Oh, the vague reality,
The mysterious certainty!
Oh, strange truth of these my guesses
In the wide thought-wildernesses!
—Truth of one divined of many flowers;
Of one raindrop in the showers
Of the long ago swift rain;
Of one tear of many tears
In some world-renownèd pain;
Of one daisy 'mid the centuries of sun;
Of a little living nun
In the garden of the years.

Yes, I am not far astray;
But I guess you as might one
Pausing when young March is grey,
In a violet-peopled day;
All his thoughts go out to places that he knew.
To his child-home in the sun,
To the fields of his regret,
To one place i' the innocent March air,

By one olive, and invent
The familiar form and scent
Safely; a white violet
Certainly is there.

Sœur Monique, remember me.
'Tis not in the past alone
I am picturing you to be;
But my little friend, my own,
In my moment, pray for me.
For another dream is mine,
And another dream is true,
      Sweeter even,
Of the little ones that shine
Lost within the light divine,—
Of some meekest flower, or you,
      In the fields of heaven.

The Garden

My heart shall be thy garden. Come, my own,
Into thy garden; thine be happy hours
Among my fairest thoughts, my tallest flowers,
From root to crowning petal thine alone.
Thine is the place from where the seeds are sown
Up to the sky enclosed, with all its showers.
But ah, the birds, the birds! Who shall build bowers
To keep these thine? O friend, the birds have flown.

For as these come and go, and quit our pine
To follow the sweet season, or, new-comers,
Sing one song only from our alder-trees,
My heart has thoughts, which, though thine eyes hold
mine,
Flit to the silent world and other summers,
With wings that dip beyond the silver seas.

Thoughts in Separation

WE never meet; yet we meet day by day
 Upon those hills of life, dim and immense—
The good we love, and sleep, our innocence.
O hills of life, high hills! And, higher than they,
Our guardian spirits meet at prayer and play.
 Beyond pain, joy, and hope, and long suspense,
 Above the summits of our souls, far hence,
An angel meets an angel on the way.

Beyond all good I ever believed of thee
 Or thou of me, these always love and live.
And though I fail of thy ideal of me,
My angel falls not short. They greet each other.
 Who knows, they may exchange the kiss we give,
Thou to thy crucifix, I to my mother.

Regrets

As, when the seaward ebbing tide doth pour
   Out by the low sand spaces,
The parting waves slip back to clasp the shore
   With lingering embraces,—

So in the tide of life that carries me
   From where thy true heart dwells,
Waves of my thoughts and memories turn to thee
   With lessening farewells;

Waving of hands; dreams, when the day forgets;
   A care half lost in cares;
The saddest of my verses; dim regrets;
   Thy name among my prayers.

I would the day might come, so waited for,
   So patiently besought,
When I, returning, should fill up once more
   Thy desolated thought;

And fill thy loneliness that lies apart
   In still, persistent pain.
Shall I content thee, O thou broken heart,
   As the tide comes again,

And brims the little sea-shore lakes, and sets
   Seaweeds afloat, and fills
The silent pools, rivers and rivulets
   Among the inland hills?

MY Fair, no beauty of thine will last
　　Save in my love's eternity.
　Thy smiles, that light thee fitfully,
Are lost for ever—their moment past—
　Except the few thou givest to me.

Thy sweet words vanish day by day,
　As all breath of mortality;
　Thy laughter, done, must cease to be,
And all thy dear tones pass away,
　Except the few that sing to me.

Hide then within my heart, O hide
　All thou art loth should go from thee.
　Be kinder to thyself and me.
My cupful from this river's tide
　Shall never reach the long sad sea.

In February

Rich meanings of the prophet-Spring adorn,
  Unseen, this colourless sky of folded showers,
  And folded winds; no blossom in the bowers;
A poet's face asleep is this grey morn.
Now in the midst of the old world forlorn
  A mystic child is set in these still hours.
  I keep this time, even before the flowers,
Sacred to all the young and the unborn:

To all the miles and miles of unsprung wheat,
  And to the Spring waiting beyond the portal,
  And to the future of my own young art,
And, among all these things, to you, my sweet,
  My friend, to your calm face and the immortal
    Child tarrying all your life-time in your heart.

San Lorenzo's Mother

I HAD not seen my son's dear face
(He chose the cloister by God's grace)
  Since it had come to full flower-time.
  I hardly guessed at its perfect prime,
That folded flower of his dear face.

Mine eyes were veiled by mists of tears
When on a day in many years
  One of his Order came. I thrilled,
  Facing, I thought, that face fulfilled.
I doubted, for my mists of tears.

His blessing be with me for ever!
My hope and doubt were hard to sever.
  —That altered face, those holy weeds.
  I filled his wallet and kissed his beads,
And lost his echoing feet for ever.

If to my son my alms were given
I know not, and I wait for Heaven.
  He did not plead for child of mine,
  But for another Child divine,
And unto Him it was surely given.

There is One alone who cannot change;
Dreams are we, shadows, visions strange;
  And all I give is given to One.
  I might mistake my dearest son,
But never the Son who cannot change.

The Love of Narcissus

L IKE him who met his own eyes in the river,
   The poet trembles at his own long gaze
That meets him through the changing nights and days
From out great Nature; all her waters quiver
With his fair image facing him for ever;
   The music that he listens to betrays
   His own heart to his ears; by trackless ways
His wild thoughts tend to him in long endeavour.

His dreams are far among the silent hills;
   His vague voice calls him from the darkened plain
With winds at night; strange recognition thrills
   His lonely heart with piercing love and pain;
He knows again his mirth in mountain rills,
   His weary tears that touch him with the rain.

A Poet of One Mood

A POET of one mood in all my lays,
   Ranging all life to sing one only love,
   Like a west wind across the world I move,
Sweeping my harp of floods mine own wild ways.
The countries change, but not the west-wind days
   Which are my songs. Most soft skies shine above,
   And on all seas the colours of a dove,
And on all fields a flash of silver greys.

I make the whole world answer to my art
   And sweet monotonous meanings. In your ears
I change not ever, bearing, for my part,
   One thought that is the treasure of my years—
A small cloud full of rain upon my heart
   And in mine arms, clasped, like a child in tears.

K

THERE's a feast undated, yet
  Both our true lives hold it fast,—
Even the day when first we met.
  What a great day came and passed,
  —Unknown then, but known at last.

And we met: You knew not me,
  Mistress of your joys and fears;
Held my hand that held the key
  Of the treasure of your years,
  Of the fountain of your tears.

For you knew not it was I,
  And I knew not it was you.
We have learnt, as days went by.
  But a flower struck root and grew
  Underground, and no one knew.

Day of days! Unmarked it rose,
  In whose hours we were to meet;
And forgotten passed. Who knows,
  Was earth cold or sunny, Sweet,
  At the coming of your feet?

One mere day, we thought; the measure
  Of such days the year fulfils.
Now, how dearly would we treasure
  Something from its fields, its rills,
  And its memorable hills.

The Young Neophyte

Who knows what days I answer for to-day?
   Giving the bud I give the flower. I bow
  This yet unfaded and a faded brow;
Bending these knees and feeble knees, I pray.
Thoughts yet unripe in me I bend one way,
   Give one repose to pain I know not now,
   One check to joy that comes, I guess not how.
I dedicate my fields when Spring is grey.

O rash! (I smile) to pledge my hidden wheat.
   I fold to-day at altars far apart
Hands trembling with what toils? In their retreat
   I seal my love to-be, my folded art.
I light the tapers at my head and feet,
   And lay the crucifix on this silent heart.

Spring on the Alban Hills

O'ER the Campagna it is dim warm weather;
   The Spring comes with a full heart silently,
 And many thoughts; a faint flash of the sea
Divides two mists; straight falls the falling feather.
With wild Spring meanings hill and plain together
   Grow pale, or just flush with a dust of flowers.
   Rome in the ages, dimmed with all her towers,
Floats in the midst, a little cloud at tether.

I fain would put my hands about thy face,
   Thou with thy thoughts, who art another Spring,
      And draw thee to me like a mournful child.
Thou lookest on me from another place;
   I touch not this day's secret, nor the thing
      That in the silence makes thy soft eyes wild.

Song of the Night at Daybreak

ALL my stars forsake me,
And the dawn-winds shake me.
Where shall I betake me?

Whither shall I run
Till the set of sun,
Till the day be done?

To the mountain-mine,
To the boughs of the pine,
To the blind man's eyne,

To a brow that is
Bowed upon the knees,
Sick with memories?

To a Daisy

SLIGHT as thou art, thou art enough to hide
Like all created things, secrets from me,
  And stand a barrier to eternity.
And I, how can I praise thee well and wide
From where I dwell—upon the hither side?
  Thou little veil for so great mystery,
  When shall I penetrate all things and thee,
And then look back? For this I must abide,

Till thou shalt grow and fold and be unfurled
Literally between me and the world.
  Then I shall drink from in beneath a spring,
And from a poet's side shall read his book.
O daisy mine, what will it be to look
  From God's side even of such a simple thing?

To One Poem in a Silent Time

WHO looked for thee, thou little song of mine?
   This winter of a silent poet's heart
  Is suddenly sweet with thee. But what thou art,
Mid-winter flower, I would I could divine.
Art thou a last one, orphan of thy line?
   Did the dead summer's last warmth foster thee?
   Or is Spring folded up unguessed in me,
And stirring out of sight,—and thou the sign?

Where shall I look—backwards or to the morrow
  For others of thy fragrance, secret child?
    Who knows if last things or if first things claim thee?
—Whether thou be the last smile of my sorrow,
  Or else a joy too sweet, a joy too wild?
    How, my December violet, shall I name thee?

OTHER EARLY POEMS

printed in *Preludes* but excluded by the author
from the *Collected Poems* of 1913; with two later
poems excluded from *Last Poems*, 1923.

To the Beloved Dead

A Lament

BELOVED, thou art like a tune that idle fingers
    Play on a window-pane.
The time is there, the form of music lingers;
    But O thou sweetest strain,
Where is thy soul? Thou liest in the wind and rain.

Even as to him who plays that idle air,
    It seems a melody,
For his own soul is full of it, so, my Fair,
    Dead, thou dost live in me,
And all this lonely soul is full of thee.

Thou song of songs!—not music as before
    Unto the outward ear;
My spirit sings thee inly evermore,
    Thy falls with tear on tear.
I fail for thee, thou art too sweet, too dear.

Thou silent song, thou ever voiceless rhyme,
    Is there no pulse to move thee,
At windy dawn, with a wild heart beating time,
    And falling tears above thee,
O music stifled from the ears that love thee?

Oh, for a strain of thee from outer air!
     Soul wearies soul, I find.
Of thee, thee, thee, I am mournfully aware,
     —Contained in one poor mind,
Who wert in tune and time to every wind.

Poor grave, poor lost belovèd! but I burn
     For some more vast To be.
As he that played that secret tune may turn
     And strike it on a lyre triumphantly,
I wait some future, all a lyre for thee.

Pygmalion

THE POET TO HIS POETRY

There is no body without its spirit or genius.—EMERSON

THOU art to live; I am watching thee.
  I have laid my patient chisel away,
And watch thee somewhat wearily.
How do I know what the mouth will say?
How do I know what the eyes will be,

—What they must be? For I suppose
The brows I made (white brows so blind),
The lovely eyelids that I chose,
Lending my hand to my inner mind,
One certain colour must enclose.

I know not what the voice will sing.
I only made the quiet breast,
And white throat with much labouring.
I only wrought and thought my best,
And lo, a new voice shall out-ring.

God knows, and knew it, fast locked in
By my own hand, who knew it not.
Have I not made the little chin,
This face and dear mouth, and begot
The voice that needs must tune within?

I am blind, I am deaf, who wrought them so,
Who loved them so. This growing one
Hath her own future there. Ah, woe!
I hardly guess what I have done.
More is gone from me than I know.

I claim the unguessed mysteries
Which make this cold white figure warm.
My life! Child, did I not devise
In dreams thy dreams, carving thy form
—Thy secrets, when I made thine eyes?

God knows. I chiselled each cold limb
With loyal pain. He has given my mind
Less light than my true hand; but dim
Is life. I wait all I shall find,
And all that I shall know, in Him.

A Tryst that Failed

Ce pauvre temps passé! : ALFRED DE MUSSET

IT was a time of wind and sun,
Morning day, and the Winter done,
Morning life, and the Spring begun.

It was a place so dreamy and brown,
Pensive with sheep-bells under the down,
Scent-dreamy, wild, with a windy crown.

You were coming, out of the Spring,
Out of the sun-dream wandering,
Out of the wind-joy hastening.

I did not see you, sweet; a flight
Of sea-birds only, pearly and white,
With a sudden shadow fled into the light.

I never heard your call, my Fair;
O music up in the flickering air!
O voice my ears so ill could spare!

And the wild, wild call my soul begot,
The long wild call, I knew not what,—
We met not then, for it reached you not,

And never again. But our hearts did greet.
Whatever path misled your feet,
Voices so true could not but meet.

Though we have strayed from that place of heather,
Your cry and mine speed on together
Above the Spring and the Summer weather.

Among the stars and in the blue,
What words could never my call may do,
—Speak my love and loss of you.

The Poets

FIRST VOICE:

OH, for the hidden songs of showers,
    And symphonies of seas!
Oh, for the secrets of a whispering wild of flowers,
    And guess'd accords of the harper-wind in the trees,
       And the warm summer-bees.
      For us the springs are old,
    And summer after summer cold.
      For us the eagles scream
    Once suddenly in the sleep of snow.
A deed is done among the centuries.
     An avalanche slides slow,
And rests: one more eternity it lies:
And there has been a fall across the dream
    Of the white sleep of snow.
Our cold and crownèd heads are lifted up in woe,
    Our barren faces,
Whose tears are sealed in awful places.
    Thou art so high above.
    Let be. A little life! a little love!
What shall repay the baffled soul, the vain endeavour?
    Not our great nights
Whose dark unmeasured windy mystery,
    Whose falls, whose heights
No heart doth feel, no eye doth see,
      For ever.
     No, Lord, no.
Nor our great open secret, snow,
Where comes the sun at even and morn
      To be alone,

And wild winds seeking solitude for their torn
　And wounded souls. Can these atone,
　　　Shall these repay?
　　No, nor the dawns we know,
Whose thoughts grow light on our eternal snow.
　　　We mourn, we pray:
　　Oh, melt our snows to rain.
　　　How can we reach thee?
　　　　Lay us low.
　Level us with the plain,
　　Oh, we beseech thee.

SECOND VOICE:

　　　O cold and glorious!
　　　O lonely and victorious!
　　Suffer your thoughts, abide.
　　Suffer, ye seven-fold tried.
Wild winds and storm, rejoice the peaks among;
　Exult with timbrel, dance, and song,
　Deafen that pain with jubilee.
　Cloud answers cloud with thunder;
And eagle's voice to eagle's voice replies far under.
　　　I cannot let you be,
　My chosen, till your answer rise to me.
　　Suffer your great wild things; abide.
　The secrets that in your abysses hide,
　　And in your desolate cold are sealed,
　Gather in heaven and fall in tender rain
That thoughts of many hearts may be revealed,
　These hearts that throng the plain.
　　Over your brows shall clouds abide,
Yours be the wildest winds, and vast suns open-eyed,
　　And crowning mists that hide
High fields of thoughts and sunlights after pain.

FIRST VOICE:

How shall we reach thee?
Level us with the plain,
Oh, we beseech thee.

To a Lost Melody

THOU art not dead, O sweet lost melody,
  Sung beyond memory,
When golden to the winds this world of ours
  Waved wild with boundless flowers;
Sung in some past when wildernesses were,—
  Not dead, not dead, lost air!
Yet in the ages long where lurkest thou,
  And what soul knows thee now?
Wert thou not given to sweeten every wind
  From that o'erburdened mind
That bore thee through the young world, and that tongue
  By which thou first wert sung?
Was not thy holy choir the endless dome,
  And nature all thy home?
Did not the warm gale clasp thee to his breast,
  Lulling thy storms to rest?
And is the June air laden with thee now,
  Passing the summer-bough?
And is the dawn-wind on a lonely sea
  Balmy with thoughts of thee?
To rock on daybreak winds dost thou rejoice,
  As first on his strong voice
Whose radiant morning soul did give thee birth,
  Gave thee to heaven and earth?
Or did each bird win one dear note of thee
  To pipe eternally?
Art thou the secret of the small field-flowers
  Nodding thy time for hours,
—Blown by the happy winds from hill to hill,
  And such a secret still?
Or wert thou rapt awhile to other spheres
  To gladden tenderer ears?

Doth music's soul contain thee, precious air,
　　　Sleepest thou clasped there,
Until a time shall come for thee to start
　　　Into some unborn heart?
Then wilt thou as the clouds of ages roll,
　　　Thou migratory soul,
Amid a different, wilder wilderness,
　　　In crowds that throng and press,
Revive thy blessed cadences forgotten
　　　In some soul new-begotten?
Oh, wilt thou ever tire of thy long rest
　　　On nature's silent breast?
And wilt thou leave thy rainbow showers, to bear
　　　A part in human care?
—Forsake thy boundless silence to make choice
　　　Of some pathetic voice?
—Forsake thy stars, thy suns, thy moons, thy skies
　　　For man's desiring sighs?

At a Poet's Grave

RATHER unto the Truth than unto one
Who sleepeth here is raised this monument.
To her he yields his tomb and is content.
Ye living singers, shower and wind and sun,

Days, nights, and flowers — obey your fancy's Art,
And mean your meanings, otherwhere; they own,
Here in this little sanctuary alone,
Meanings beyond the deepest poet's heart.

Sing through the world; this is another world,
This poet's empire, but he will not claim
One flower sprung from his heart, nor ever steep

One with his thoughts; his thoughts in truth are furled.
There was no need of him; hush up his fame,
Now earth has laid her docile child to sleep.

The Poet to Nature

I HAVE no secrets from thee, lyre sublime,
My lyre whereof I make my melody.
I sing one way like the west wind through thee,
With my whole heart, and hear thy sweet strings chime.

But thou, who soundest in my tune and rhyme,
Hast tones I wake not, in thy land and sea,
Loveliness not for me, secrets from me,
Thoughts for another, and another time.

And as, the west wind passed, the south wind alters
His intimate sweet things, his hues of noon,
The voices of his waves, sound of his pine,

The meanings of his lost heart—this thought falters
In my short song: 'Another bard shall tune
Thee, my one Lyre, to other songs than mine.'

The Poet to his Childhood

IN my thought I see you stand with a path on either hand,
Hills that look into the sun, and there a river'd meadow-
  land.
And your lost voice with the things that it decreed across
  me thrills,
    When you thought, and chose the hills.

'If it prove a life of pain, greater have I judged the gain.
With a singing soul for music's sake, I climb and meet the
  rain,
And I choose, whilst I am calm, my thought and labouring
  to be
    Unconsoled by sympathy.'

But how dared you use me so? For you bring my ripe years
  low
To your child's whim and a destiny your child-soul could
  not know.
And that small voice legislating I revolt against, with tears.
    But you mark not, through the years.

'To the mountain leads my way. If the plains are green to-
  day,
These my barren hills are flushing faintly, strangely in the
  May,
With the presence of the Spring amongst the smallest
  flowers that grow.'
    But the summer in the snow?

Do you know, who are so bold, how in sooth the rule will
    hold,
Settled by a wayward child's ideal at some ten years old?
—How the human hearts you slip from, thoughts and love
    you stay not for,
            Will not open to you more?

You were rash then, little child, for the skies with storms
    are wild,
And you faced the dim horizon with its whirl of mists, and
    smiled,
Climbed a little higher, lonelier, in the solitary sun,
            To feel how the winds came on.

But your sunny silence there, solitude so light to bear,
Will become a long dumb world up in the colder sadder
    air,
And the little mournful lonelinesses in the little hills
            Wider wilderness fulfils.

And if e'er you should come down to the village or the
    town,
With the cold rain for your garland, and the wind for your
    renown,
You will stand upon the thresholds with a face of dumb
    desire,
            Nor be known by any fire.

It is memory that shrinks. You were all too brave, me-
    thinks,
Climbing solitudes of flowering cistus and the thin wild
    pinks,
Musing, setting to a haunting air in one vague reverie
            All the life that was to be.

With a smile do I complain in the safety of the pain,
Knowing that my feet can never quit their solitudes again;
But regret may turn with longing to that one hour's choice
  you had,
      When the silence broodeth sad.

I rebel *not*, child gone by, but obey you wonderingly,
For you knew not, young rash speaker, all you spoke, and
  now will I,
With the life, and all the loneliness revealed that you
  thought fit,
      Sing the Amen, knowing it.

A Study

In three monologues, with interruptions

I

BEFORE LIGHT

AMONG the first to wake. What wakes with me?
A blind wind and a few birds and a star.
With tremor of darkened flowers and whisper of birds,
Oh, with a tremor, with a tremor of heart—
Begins the day i' the dark. I, newly waked,
Grope backwards for my dreams, thinking to slide
Back unawares to dreams, in vain, in vain.
There is a sorrow for me in this day.
It watched me from afar the livelong night,
And now draws near, but has not touched me yet.
In from my garden flits the secret wind,—
My garden.—This great day with all its hours
(Its hours, my soul!) will be like other days
Among my flowers. The morning will awake,
Like to the lonely waking of a child
Who grows uneasily to a sense of tears,
Because his mother had come and wept and gone;
The morning grass and lilies will be wet,
In all their happiness, with mysterious dews.
And I shall leave the high noon in my garden,
The sun enthroned and all his court my flowers,
And go my journey as I live,—alone.
Then in the ripe rays of the later day
All the small blades of thin grass one by one,
Looked through with sun, will make each a long shade,
And daisies' heads will bend with butterflies.
And one will come with secrets at her heart,
Evening, whose darkening eyes hide all her heart,
And poppy-crowned move 'mid my lonely flowers.

And shall another, I wonder, come with her—
I, with a heavy secret at my heart,
Uncrowned of all crowns, to my garden and flowers?
Thou little home of mine, fair be thy day.
These things will be, but oh, across the hills,
Behind me in the dark, what things will be?
—Well, even if sorrow fills me through and through
Until my life be pain and pain my life,
Shall I not bear myself and my own life?
—A little life, O Lord, a little sorrow.
And I remember once when I was ill
That the whole world seemed breaking through with me,
Who lay so light and still; stillness availed not,
My weakness being a thing of power, I thought.

'Come to the Port to-morrow', says the letter,
And little more, except a few calm words,
Intended to prepare me (and I guess,
I guess for what). He never was too kind,
This man, the one i' the world, kin to my son,
Who knew my crime, who watched me with cold eyes,
And stayed me with calm hands, and hid the thing,
For horror more than pity; and took my son;
And mercifully let me ebb away
In this grey town of undesigned grey lives,
Five years already. To-day he sends for me.
And now I will prevent the dawn with prayers.

2

ABOUT NOON

She shut her five years up within the house.
And towards the noon she lifted up her eyes,
Looked to the gentle hills with a stirred heart,
Moved with the mystery of unknown places,

Near to a long-known home; smiled, as she could,
A difficult smile that hurt half of her mouth,
Until she passed the streets and all sharp looks.

'Sharp looks, and since I was a child, sharp looks!
These know not, certainly, who scan me so,
That not a girl of all their brightest girls
Has such an eager heart for smiles as I.
It is no doubt the fault of my cold face
And reticent eyes that never make appeal,
Or plead for the small pale bewildered soul.
If they but knew what a poor child I am!
—Oh, born of all the past, what a poor child!
I could waste golden days and showers of words,
And laugh for nothing, and read my poets again,
And tend a voice I had, songless for ever;—
I would not if I might. I would not cease,
Not if I might, the penance and the pain
For that lost soul down somewhere in the past,
That soul of mine that did and knew such things,
If I could choose; and yet I wish, I wish,
Such little wishes, and so longingly.
Who would believe me, knowing what I am?

'Now from these noontide hills my home, my time,
My life for years lies underneath mine eyes,
And all the years that led up to these years.
I can judge now, and not the world for me.
And I, being what I am, and having done
What I have done, look back upon my youth
—Before my crime, I mean,—and testify:
It was not happy, no, it was not white,
It was not innocent, no, the young fair time.
The people and the years passed in my glass;

And all the insincerity of my thoughts
I laid upon the pure and simple Nature
(Now all the hills and fields are free of me),
Smiling at my elaborate sigh the smile
Of any Greek composing sunny gods.
And now begins my one true white child-time,
This time of desolate altars and all ruins.
For Pan is dead and the altars are in ruins.

'The world is full of endings for me, I find,
Emotions lost, and words and thoughts forgotten.
Yet amid all these *last* things, there is one,
But one Beginning, a seed within my soul.
Come quickly! and go by quickly, O my years!
Strip me of things and thoughts; as I have seen
The ilex changing leaves; for day by day
A little innocent life grows in my life,
A little ignorant life i' the world-worn life;
And I become a child with a world to learn,
Timorous, with another world to learn,
Timorous, younger, whiter towards my death.'

She turned to the strange sea that five long years
Had sent her letters of his misty winds,
Bearing a cry of storms in other lands,
And songs of mariners singing over seas;
And having long conjectured of his face,
Seeing his face, paused, thinking of the past.
Down the hills came she to the town and sea,
And met her child's friend where he waited her.
She swayed to his words unsaid, as the green canes
Murmur i' the quiet unto a wind that comes:

'I sent for you, mind, for your sake alone.
—No, my dear ward is well. But it has chanced
(I know it's a hard thing for you to bear,
But you are strong, I know) that he has learnt
What I had faithfully kept,—your life, your past,
Your secret. Well, we hope that you repent,
At least, your son and I.'

                        'God bless my son,
My little son hopes I repent at least.'

'When he had read the papers—by mischance—
I would have kept them from him, broken down,
Beside himself at first, though the young heart
Recovered and is calm now, he resolved
On the completest parting, for he thinks
He could not live under one sky with you.
But being unwilling to disturb you now
And vex you in your harmless life, gives up
His hopes in England, his career, and sails
To-night to make a new life in the States.
As to the question of your seeing him
(He is in the town here), I persuaded him
To let you choose, this being probably
The last time in this world. It rests with you.'

'I pray you, as we pray morning and night,
Save me from the sick eyes of my one child;
But let me see my one child once. Amen.

'I never came across the hills before
In all these years; now all these years are done.
Who would have said it, yesterday at this hour?
Now my son knows, and I have crossed the hills,

And sure my poor face faces other things.
Not back! not home! anything, anything,
Anything—no, don't turn, I am very calm.
Not back the way I came to-day, not home.
Oh, anything but home and a long life.'

'Am I the arbiter? Besides, what fate
Can you desire more merciful than home
And hidden life? And then remember him.
You have borne the separation as it seems
With the most perfect patience. And your life
Ending (as to the world), owes this at least—·
It is not much—to his bright beginning life,
Absence and perfect silence till you die.
I've done my duty, as I think, to both.
If you seemed in the least to ask for pity
I well could pity you. I hope that time
Will bring you a softer heart. Good-bye.'

'Good-bye.'

3

AT TWILIGHT

Gone, O my child forsaking me, my flower.
Yet I forsaken pity you with tears,
Gone while I learn a world to learn a world.
I am to have no part with you again,
And you have many things to share; it's keen,—
I love you, I love you; but more keen is this,—
That you will have no part with me again;
And what have I to share? Pain, happy child.
Gone, gone into the west, for ever gone,
O little one, my flower; not you alone,

My son who are leaving me, but he, the child
Of five years back. That is the worst farewell.
I had not thought him lost until to-day.
But he had kept with me until to-day;—
Never seen, never heard; but he was there,
Behind the door on which I laid my hand,
Out in the garden when I sat within,
A turn of road before me in my walks.
As others greet a presence I did greet
An absence, O my sweet, my sweet surprise!
How will it be now! for he is so changed
I hardly knew the face I saw pass by.
And yet it is the one that must of needs
Grow from that long ago face innocent,
Grave with the presage of a human life.
So, child, giving again in thought my kiss,
My last, long since, I kiss you tall and changed
In that one kiss, and kiss you a man and old,
And so I kiss you dead. And yet, O child,
O child, a certain soul goes from my days;
They fall together like a rosary told,
Not aves now, but beads,—you being gone.

I was not worthy to be comfortless,
I find, and feasts broke in upon my fasts;
And innocent distractions and desires
Surprised me in my penitential tears.
For my absent child God gives me a child in Spring;
New seasons and the fresh and innocent earth,
Ever new years and children of the years,
Kin to the young thoughts of my weary heart,
Chime with the young thoughts of my weary heart,
My kin in all the world. And He Himself
Is young i' the quiet time of cold and snows.

(Mary! who fledst to Egypt with Him; Joseph!
And thou whose tomb I kissed in Padua,
Protect this perilous childhood in my heart!)
But oh, to-night, I know not why, to-night
Out of the earth and sky, out of the sea
My consolations fade. These empty arms
I stretch no more unto the beautiful world,
But clasp them close about the lonely heart
No other arms will clasp. What is thy pain,
What is thy pain, inexplicable heart?
Sorrow for ruined and for desolate days.
Failing in penitence, I, who fail in all,
Leave all my thoughts alone, and lift mine eyes
Quietly to One who makes amends for me.
Peace, O my soul, for thou hast failed in all:
(One thought, at last, that I might take to Heaven!)

It's well I never guessed this thing before,—
I mean the weakness and the littleness
Of that which by God's grace begins in me.
Oh, earthly hopes and wishes, stay with me.
(He will be patient); linger, O my loves
And phases of myself, and play with this
New life of grace (as He whose gift it is
Played with the children, a child). How could I bear
To see how little is perfect yet—a speck
If all things else should suddenly wither away?
(And yet they wither away, they wither away.)
Less than I knew, less than I know am I,
Returning childless, but, O Father, a child.

She therefore turned unto the Eastern hills,
Thrilled with a west wind sowing stars. She saw
Her lonely upward way climb to the verge

And ending of the day-time; and she knew
The downward way in presence of the night.
She heard the fitful sheep-bells in the glen
Move like a child's thoughts. There she felt the earth
Lonely in space. And all things suddenly
Shook with her tears. She went with shadowless feet,
Moving along the shadow of the world,
Faring alone to home and a long life,
Setting a twilight face to meet the stars.

To Two Travellers

From VICTOR HUGO

COME soon, my friends, poet and painter, both.
I need you always, and my eyes are loth
    To miss your gentle faces.
With idle touches on the strings and quills,
My sad lyre traces you through plains and hills,
    Towns and historic places.

My music is gone with you overseas.
O lute and pencil, come and give me ease,
    For you have stolen my art.
I thirst for thee, thou double stream most sweet,
Alpheus and Arethuse, whose waters fleet
    Met, mingled in my heart.

I watch the painter and the poet linger
In some brown street, and trace with learned finger
    The ogives of a door,
Or turn delighted, at a whim, to chase
The gleam of dark eyes and a lovely face
    Flashed from an upper floor.

Of the young girl, and of the ruin hoary,
Paint thou the beauty, and sing thou the story.
    Love all, divine and human.
Piercing through wall and veil, your eyes can see
Within the temple closed the Deity,
    And love within the woman.

177

M

My brother, my apostle! Brother and brother!
One paints the lovely universe; the other
     Explains it with a word.
Each has the part he loves. Painter, the whole
Fair world for thee; poet, for thee the soul;
     For each, for both, the Lord!

CLOUDS are mingled in changing grey:
A rainy morning in spring—so be it.
There'll be no revel of roses and may;
Go back, children who came to see it.
There'll be no noon on the hills to-day;

No deep sky lost in the sun, but rain;
No clouds like light in a light that is greater.
The young sky weeps in a youth of pain,
And though the sweet sun may send us later
Long glories over the level plain,

Yet there are slopes of the Eastern lawn
Among the hills—those morning places,
With souls to the early time up-drawn;
With tremulous dews and dreamy faces
Set to the fresh thoughts of the dawn—

Set to the innocent airs, and sweet
Long sunshine of the morning only.
Though the far plain of wood and wheat
Shine rainbow-robed, their shadows, lonely,
Will darken the country about their feet.

The sun may break: we will thank God for it,
In a long bright evening—who shall say?
The dark veil fall; but the morning wore it.
And many flowers will have done their day,
And many birds will have died before it.

'WHEN have I known a boy
    Kinder than this my daughter, or his kiss
More filial, or the clasping of his joy
    Closer than this?'

Thus did a mother think;
And yet her daughter had been long away,
Estranged, on other business; but the link
    Was fast to-day.

This mother, who was she?
I know she was the earth, she was the land.
Her daughter, a gay girl, toiled happily,
    Sheaves in her hand.

Aenigma Christi

'Videmus nunc in aenigmate'

NONE can be like Him, none!
In love? In grief? Nay, man's capacity,
Rifled unto its depths, is reached, is done—
    Christ's, an unfathomed sea.

    None can be like Him, none;
Not she who bore Him. Yet I saw the whole
Eternal, infinite Christ within the one
    Small mirror of her soul.

VERY EARLY POEMS

written in 1869 and never printed by the author but
included in the *Oxford* edition of 1940

Song of the Soul of the Organ
The Poet to her Poet

PLAY, lest thy soul should break O organ-player.
Thy harmonies have strength that shall up-bear
The pale and faltering thoughts of many a prayer.

Thou shalt unfurl them in a quiet place
That love and meekness make for thee, a space
Of twilight for the shining of thy face;

Calm place where those who love thee come and go,
But where I wait thee who do love thee so,
And where the touches of thy hands I know;

And know how they did tremble in such an air,
And what thy doubts and what thy changes were.
—Thou tread'st me underfoot O organ-player,

In those far tones more known and felt than heard,
The great quiet sea-deeps of the soul being stirred
That never live in storm or wake in word.

I alone shudder and moan to thy great things,
O wildly loved! and clasp thy sufferings
With arms of music cast about thy wings.

Thro' all thy meanings, all, come draw me higher.
Up to thy summit music I aspire.
Draw me. Lo, I would break, for thy desire.

Wind-Song to the Hill

The Poet sings to a Maiden

How shall I climb thee, hill of flowers and clover?
—I muse with cloud-wings furled against the sun.
A pause too still for earth hath stolen over.
In the divine quiet, Nature, little one,
Draws breath before the coming of thy lover.

Say, shall I come with wings from plains of flowers
Where poets' thoughts make a rain-bow wilderness?
Shall I bring songs from where the diamond showers
And grey skies mix the sun with tenderness?
And shall the souls of many larks be ours?

Or shall I tell thee of the midmost wailing
Of an indignant and unpitied sea?
Wet thee with what did wet me of the unfailing
Long wave-despairs that fare forsakenly,
Passion with pain that follows unavailing?

Over the round hill-tops shall I come to thee,
High-hearted, with light feet upon the thyme,
A child, an impulse sprung from spring to woo thee,
Young with all youth, O hill that I would climb,
With morning thoughts from Morning throned to sue
thee?

Shall I rend clouds for garments to enfold thee,
Bind round thy brows the bent and crying skies?
Darkened with my dark hours shall I behold thee
Through all the great rains of my passionate eyes?
With arms of pain and tempest shall I hold thee?

Shall I come cold with news of dawn, o'ertaking
The tired stars? From my soul's sleep shall I call
Things that we guess not?—as the bird half-waking
Sings out of dreams those deepest songs of all
From some unknown sleep-heaven i' the dark
   day-breaking?

Shall I be all but silence, fitfully failing
Flickering in pale air like a dying light?
Shall I come as the west wind cometh, trailing
The day's gold robes thro' half the heavenly night,
Till round thy brows all the cold east is paling?

Or shall I be the fervid South-wind for thee?
Summer-long thro' the sunlights shall I stream?
Swift, but serene as beauty blow before thee,
Move among all the still stars with my dream,
Bring souls of deep South-summers to adore thee?

Shall I storm, love-strong, thy small wildernesses,
Thy humble heights, bare to all suns and showers?
Sport with thy timorous thoughts and poet-guesses,
Shaking thy shortest grass and little flowers,
Rioting in thy dreamiest lonelinesses?

—Or loiter where thy longest lawn reposes,
Where the dim plain is gentlest from thy feet,
Wait thy slow sweetness, watch as it uncloses,
Tarry thy silence, quiet with pale June heat,
Wait for the opening of thy wan wild roses?

—Oh, with a pæan of sound I will renown thee,
With waves of lights and shadows I will drown thee.
And like a wind, a wild wind I will crown thee.

To a reader who should love me

Come in the year's mid-summer and in thine,
Into the deep soft midnight for a space,
'Mong wild closed flowers and wheat, a meek tilled place
Of folded poppies, maize, and rills of vine.
There, young and mournful, in this realm of mine,
With only a little growing grass for thy face,
Only the labouring earth for thine embrace
All my young heart shall sing for thee and shine;
A nightingale and loneliest of fire-flies
Palpitate in the darkness light and strain,
Tho' thine own stars be stifled in soft skies,
And thine own music mute, for any pain.
And I have dews to wet thy quiet eyes
Till thou forsake me for thy life again.

A Cenotaph

Thy life is lonely utterly
O one I know of emptied days!
A place of wakeful pain for me,
Remote by consecrated ways,—
If I could only die in thee.

We are apart, whose hands clung so.
We might have lived—I mourn with thee.
Sweet life was not for us to know.
We cannot die till death shall be.
Lament thy love, and let me go.

Yet patient rebel that thou art,
All thy quiet life awaits me now,
In a world of thoughts that lies apart.
Are we not thoughts ourselves, sayest thou,
Shall distance keep us heart from heart?

Thy white hours clad as mourners all
With faces to the ground go by.
And sweet decorous tears do fall
Since we were parted, thou and I,
In one long feast of funeral.

Thy thoughts have made a silentness
Because thy music is away,
That they may fold themselves and guess
The lost airs in the silent day.
And they are pale with tenderness.

O blessed thoughts! O holy hours!
No place is fairer under heaven
With diamond dews and emerald showers,
Than this of mine that thou hast given,
No warmer winds, no taller flowers.—

And yet I have not reached mine end.
How shall I die, although I have
Thy love, thy tears to mourn me and tend?
Lo thou hast made an exquisite grave
And I am living O my Friend,

And run to all the winds that call.
Sweet are the thoughts, O loneliest
Thou glorifiest me withal,—
My subjects—if I could but rest
And die the quiet queen of them all.

And all thy flowers beneath the rain
Are happy memories thou dost keep.
Mine eyes closed in them, for thy pain,
And like a child's that feigneth sleep,
When I forgot, unclosed again.

Thy far life is no place for me.
Oh lay thy great love under the flowers
—Unless an angel pitying thee
Having no need of the live hours
Lies in the place where I should be.

On Keats's Grave

*He said that the greatest delight of his life had
been to watch the growth of flowers. And when dying
'I feel them growing over me'.*

THEY waited not for showers
But made a garden in the dark above him,
—Stayed not for summer, growing things that love him.

Beyond the light, beyond the hours,
Behind the wind, where Nature thinks the flowers,
He entered in his dying wandering.
And daisies infantine were thoughts of his,
And different grasses solved his mysteries.
He lived in flowers a snatch of spring,
And had a dying longing that uncloses
In wild white roses.

Down from the low hills with pines
Into the fields at rest, the summer done,
I went by pensive ways of tombs and vines
To where the place I dream of is;
And in a stretch of meditative sun
Cloven by the dark flames of the cypresses
Came to the small grave of my ended poet.
—I had felt the wild things many a dreamy hour
Pushing above him from beyond the sea,
But when I saw it
It chanced there was no flower;
And that was, too, a silent time for me.

O life of blossoms—Proserpine!
O time of flowers where art thou now,

And in what darkness movest thou?
In the lost heart of this quiet poet of mine
So well-contented with his growth of flowers?
Beyond the suns and showers
Stirrest thou in a silence that begets
The exquisite thought, the tuneful rhyme?
The first intention of the violets,
And the beginnings of the warm wild-thyme?
Indeed the poets do know
A place of thoughts where no winds blow,
And not a breath is sighing,
Beyond the light, beyond the hours,
Where all a summer of enchanted flowers
Do mark his place, his dying.
Sweet life, and is it there thy sceptre passes
On long arrays of flowering grasses
And rows of crimson clover?
Are these the shades thou reignest over?

Come ere the year forgets
The summer, her long lover.
O Proserpine, November violets!

—Where art thou now?
And in what darkness movest thou
Who art in life the life of melodies?
Within the silent living poet's heart
Where no song is,
Where, every one apart,
Arrays of the morne fancies err
Vaguer than pain in sleep, vaguer than pain,
And no winds stir;—
Over these shadows dost thou reign?

See now, in this still day
All winds are strayed and lost, wandered away,
Everywhere from Soracte to the sea.
All singing things muse in the sun,
And trees of fragrant leaves do happily
Meditate in their sweet scents every one,
The pæans done.
All olives turn and dream in grey at ease,
Left by the silver breeze.
Long smiles have followed the peal of mirth.
—But silence has no place for me,
A silent singer on earth.

Awake!
And thro' the sleeping season break,
With young new shoots for this young poet's sake,
With singing lives for all these dreams of mine,
O darkened Proserpine!
Out of the small grave and the thoughts I love
Stir thou in me and move,
If haply a song of mine may seem a dim
Sweet flower grown over him.
Oh come from underground and be
Flowers for my young dear poet and songs for me.

POEMS FIRST COLLECTED
1946

The 'Sunderland Children' was printed in
'Merry England', 1883; the translation in
the 'Pall Mall Gazette', 1897.

The Sunderland Children

*On the 183 Sunderland children who lost their lives in
a panic at the Victoria Hall, 16th June, 1883*

THIS was the surplus childhood, held as cheap!
  Not worth the care which shields
The lambs that are to stay, the corn to reap—
  The promise of the fields.

The nation guards her future. Fruits and grass
  And vegetable life
Are fostered league by league. But oh, the mass
  Of childhood over-rife!

O mass, O units! Oh, the separate story
  Planned for each breather of breath!
This futile young mankind, and transitory,
  Is left to stray to Death.

O promise, presage, menace! Upon these
  A certain seal is laid.
Unkept, unbroken, are the auguries
  These little children made.

For threat is bound with promise; and the nation
  Holds festival of regret
Over these dead—dead in their isolation—
  Wisely. She feared their threat.

Misfortune

(translated from Ada Negri)

ARMED, and with lightning eyes that clove the dark,
  One stood at midnight near me.
Told me her daunting name, and claimed me: 'Hark!
  I am Misfortune. Fear me!'

'I shall not leave thy pathway, nor forsake,
  Young one, thy timorous side;
Shall watch thy sleep, and on thy grave shall wake.'
  'Let me alone,' I cried.

Yet she kept near: 'By unrebuked decrees
  Thou art made a flower of snow,
A dusty flower, a flower of cypress trees,
  Of mire, of fire, of woe.'

I cried, 'I am for life, for joy, for one,
  Only one fear—love's own.
I want the kiss of genius and the sun,'
  I wept, 'Let me alone!'

'Glory,' she said, 'is of my gift; renown
  Closes my troubled day.
I crush and I proclaim, I wound, I crown.'
  I said, 'Misfortune, stay!'